The Muslims of India on the Crossroad of Faith

Akram Mohammad

Dedication

To my late parents, Father Major. M. Mustafa (Rtd. Indian Army officer) and Mother Mrs. Kulsoom Begum, who planted the seed of knowledge in my mind and nurtured it. They said, "Words have the power to change the world."

Greatly loved and deeply missed the source of inspiration, guidance, and support of my late brother Dr. M. Mukarram, Ph.D. (AMU), late father-in-law CMO Dr. M. Shoeb Alam Khan, MBBS, MD., and my late sister Mrs. I Nasimun I Nisa I Farhat, BA, B.Ed. (AMU), M.A (BHU).

Acknowledgment

I, Dr. Akram Mohammad, Ph.D. (Chem.), LL.M., am extremely grateful to my family for encouraging me in all my pursuits and inspiring me to follow my dreams. I am grateful to my wife, daughters, and sons, who supported me emotionally and financially to make it possible to complete my book.

Also, I would like to acknowledge my family; my wife Mrs. Nuzhat Alam Akram, B.A, Ph. A. (Ottawa); daughters, Miss Afreenish Yusirah Akram, B.Sc, food Science, M.A.(Carleton University, Ottawa); Miss Parihan Israh Akram, B.Sc. Health Science (Carleton University, Ottawa); Miss.Afrah Inshirah Akram grade- 5, Std, and Sons, Azfar Al-Affan Akram, B.Sc-Biotechnology, M.Sc.Std. (University of Ottawa), Yawar Az-Farhan Akram, B.Sc.-Biotechnology, Std. (University of Ottawa), Zafar Eshan Akram, B.Sc. Neuroscience Std. (Carleton University), Uzair Ziad Akram, grade -12 Std.

Thanks to my Indian family members, brothers, Col. Dr. M. Azam, M.D., Ph.D.; Dr.M. Muazzam, M.Tech., Ph.D.; Prof. Dr. M. Aslam-Hameshgul, MD; Advocate Farhat Ashfaque, LL.B. and Principal M. Samiullah, M.Com., Capt. Shabir, Capt. Ishrar Ahmed, Ibrar Ahmed and Mahmood Khan, and M. Faizan, Arshlan, Shiraz, Shuja, Nazia, Rubina, Yashmin, Ehtisham, Kashish, and Khubaib.

Thanks to my mother-in-law, Mrs. Najma Khatoon, sisters-in-law, Mrs. Rafat Alam and Mrs. Farhat Alam, and brother-in-law, Intekhab Alam.

Thanks to my late father, Major M. Mustafa; late mother, Mrs. Kulsoom Begum; late brother, Dr.M. Mukarram; late sisters, Mrs.

Nasimun Nisa Farhat, Shabnam Mustafa and Razia Mustafa, and late father-in-law CMO Dr. M. Shoeb Alam khan.

Thanks to all my friends, family, relatives, and teachers for continuously inspiring and providing me with moral support to complete my dream.

Thanks to my friends from school, university, and professional time, Prof. Shahabuddin, Late Irfan Ahmed, Dr. Salman Siddiqui, Eng. Firoz Nomani, Adv. Ishtiyaq Siddiqui, Dr. Asif Zameer Lari, Prof. Manmohan Gupta, Pervez Akhtar, Dist. Judge Pradeep Pant, Adv. Anil Mishra, Eng. Neel Kamal Singh, Pradeep Agrawal, Hari Prakash Gupta, Vijay Gupta, Eng. Abdul Hassan, Rajkumar Gupta, Dr. Ibrahim, Prof. Mobin Siddiqui, FRSC, Adv. Hurmal, Eng. Javed, Lib. Khursheed Ahmed. Br. Aurangzeb Alam Ballia, Late Dr. Manuwar Ali Khan, Dr. Haroon Khan, Dr. Tariq Khan, Dr. Parwaiz Khalid, Dr. Shamshad Alam, Dr. Yamin Siddiqui, Prof. Kalbe Javed, Eng Wiquar Husain, Dr. Serdal Sevinc, Prof. Luqman Khan, Zahid Siddiqi, Eng. Nasir Shahin, Eng Amjad Khan, Dr. Imran Ishrat, Rehan Shaikh, Br. Neyaz Shaheen, Br. Hameed Udeen, Imam Khalil, Dr. Arshad Siddiqui, Br. Abdullah Aden, Dr. Shoeb Mustafa Khan. Br. Qaswar, Br. Omar Sher, Yakhlaqu Hussain, Abdul Qaudir, Dr. Masood Khan, Dr. Arif Khan, Dr. Shahzad Shamdani, Eng Tauseef Irfan, Prof. Atique Ahmed. Dr. Raghib Husain, Dr. Razaur Rehman, Br. Zafar Azamgarh, Br. Mirza Abdul Qaiyum, Prof. J.K. Srivastva, Dr. U Singha, Viswanath Reddy, Eng. Arshad Ahmed, Prof. Abbas Ali Mehdi KGMU.

Thanks to my teachers Prof. Firoz Ahmed (AMU), Dr. Onkar Tripathi (CDRI), Dr. Abdul Mujeeb Kidwai (ITRC), Prof. B.B. Pande-Law (LU), Dr. Rick Moody and Dr Saeed Qureshi, (Health Canada), Prof. Edward Lai (Carleton University), Late Prof. Jack Carnet, Prof

Ian Clark, Prof. Liam, Prof James Gomes, Prof Ajoy Basak, Prof Mad Karen. (University of Ottawa). Dr. Max Arela (Montreal University), Late Prof. Tahir Hussain (St. John University), Dr. Raphael Galea (NRC).

Thanks to Mrs. Nuzhat Alam Akram for financial support.

Thanks to the book project team members for helping me publish this book.

About the Author

Dr. Akram Mohammad, Ph.D. (Chem.), LL.M., is the author of the book "The Muslim of India on the Crossroad of Faith."

Dr. Akram graduated with a Ph.D. (Chemistry) from Aligarh Muslim University, Aligarh, India; an LL.M. from Lucknow University, India, and an M.Sc. in Accelerator Mass Spectrometry (AMS) from the University of Ottawa, Canada. He completed a post-graduate diploma course in Regulatory Affairs from AAPS, Toronto, and Paralegal studies from ACA, Ottawa.

He worked for his M.Phil. and Ph.D. Research thesis from Central Drug Research Institute (CDRI), Lucknow, and worked as a Research Associate at Industrial Toxicology Research Centre (ITRC), Lucknow, India. He was awarded a fellowship from the Council of Scientific and Industrial Research (CSIR), Delhi, and the Indian Council of Medical Research (ICMR), Delhi. He wrote an LL.M. thesis on "Crime against women." He was President of the

Research Scientist and Fellow Association (RSFA), Lucknow. He was an advocate and member of the Delhi Bar Council, India. He is the founder of "Micro Library with Micro Funding" in India, which serves humanity and society.

Mohammad was a scientist at the FAO of UNO in the Ministry of Agriculture and Water research lab, NAWRC, Riyadh, Saudi Arabia.

He also served as the Professor, Chairman, and Head of Exam. Board at College of Pharmacy, Qassim University, Saudi Arabia.

He was a scientific researcher in Health Canada, Ottawa. He discovered and developed flow through diffusion cells, a device to measure toxic chemicals in human skin.

He was also a research and teaching associate at Carleton University, the National Research Council (NRC), and the University of Ottawa, Canada.

Dr. Akram was born in Army Hospital, Madras, T.N., India, and grew up in their paternal grandparents' home, Jamuwawu, Bilthraroad, Ballia, UP, and maternal grandparents' home, Khairaty, Sivan-Chapra, Bihar, India. Presently, he lives with his family in Nepean, Ottawa, Ontario, Canada.

He got his primary, high school, and university educations from Jamuwawu, Ballia; Jabalpur, M.P., Allahabad, U.P., Bilthraroad-Ballia, Aligarh Muslim University, Aligarh; Lucknow University, India, and the University of Ottawa Canada.

Major M. Mustafa, the author's late father, was an Indian Army Officer, and his late mother, Mrs. Kulsoom Begum, was the family manager. Dr. Akram has four brothers, Col.Dr. Azam, Dr.

Muazzam, late Dr. Mukarram, Prof.Aslam, and late sisters Mrs. Nasimun Nisa Farhat, late Miss. Shabnam Mustafa, and late Miss Razia Mustafa.

His home was in Bilthraroad, Ballia. He got married in Azamgarh to Nuzhat Alam daughter of CMO. Dr. M. Shoeb Alam and Mrs. Najma Khatoon from Baheri, Ballia, India. Dr. Akram has three daughters, Afreenish, Parihan, and Afrah, and four sons, Azfar, Yawar, Zafar, and Uzair. He now lives with his family at 347 Bakewell Crescent, Barrhaven, Nepean, Ottawa, K2G 7E9 Ontario, Canada. Dr. Akram's contact email: is mnakram100@gmail.com

Preface

In today's world, where the ideals of justice, morality, and fraternity often appear obscured by the shadows of injustice, corruption, and conflict, it becomes imperative to pause and engage in profound reflection. One might as well trace down their roots. This book emerges as a beacon amidst the tumult, offering a comprehensive exploration of the essence of our shared humanity.

As we navigate the complexities of societal norms, it becomes increasingly apparent that the fundamental principles of justice and morality have frequently been distorted by those occupying positions of power. Yet, notwithstanding the myriad intricacies that characterize our modern world, there exists within each individual a moral compass—a conscience—that steadfastly guides us toward what is righteous and just.

The following pages unravel the intricacies of history and tradition, shedding light on the evolution of our societies and the consequential role played by religion therein. While religion, in its purest form, has historically served as a source of solace and moral guidance, it has, regrettably, been manipulated into a divisive tool, fostering discord rather than fostering unity.

However, amidst the chaos and disarray, this book transcends religious boundaries to elucidate the universal values of compassion, empathy, and a resolute commitment to the collective well-being of all members of society. I look forward to igniting a spark within each reader—a spark that illuminates the path toward a more tranquil and prosperous existence. It is my earnest hope that this book serves as a gentle reminder of the inherent goodness that resides within each of us, irrespective of our particular creed or belief system.

As we embark on this journey of introspection and enlightenment, may this book serve as a guiding beacon, illuminating the path toward a future characterized by unity, compassion, and the enduring triumph of the human spirit.

With profound sincerity and humility,

Akram Mohammad.

Contents

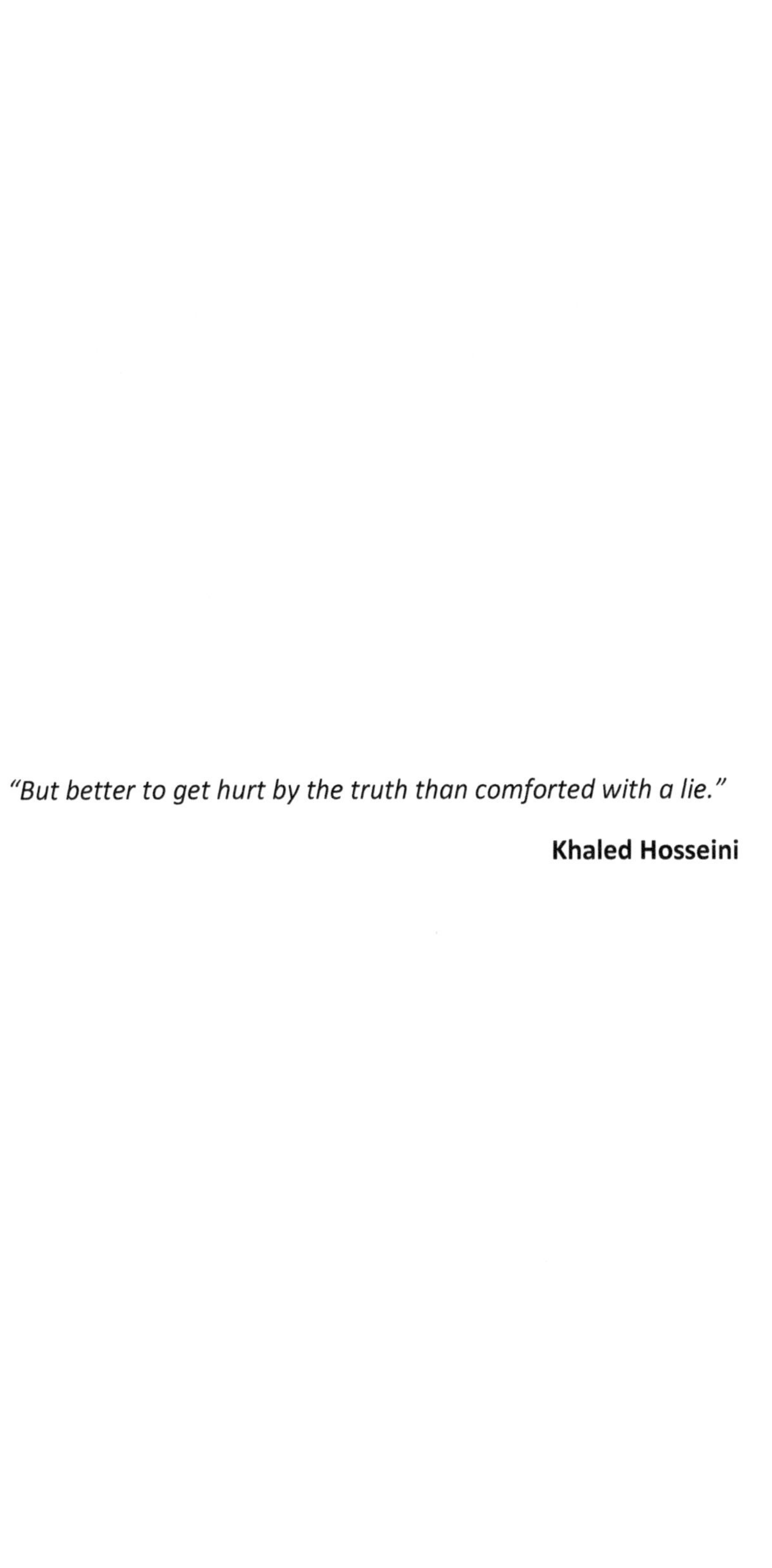

"But better to get hurt by the truth than comforted with a lie."

Khaled Hosseini

Introduction

The rules of the game were always the same. In other words, virtues such as equality, justice, and morality were always present in every nation on earth. As humans, it is our responsibility to live a life based on that *moral* compass. But despite being the species gifted with speech and intelligence, we are the easiest to get distracted by injustice, corruption, and crime.

Humans are blessed with something called 'conscience,' the innate sense of what is right and what is wrong. If nothing else, it is this single aspect that gives us an upper hand over the other species in Kingdom Animalia. The good news is we are proud of *this* conscience. The bad news is we know very well how to exploit it.

Indeed, we have come a long way since the Stone Age. From applauding a mere line carved on stones to grand inaugurations of the latest iPhone, a lot has happened in between. There is no exact point of origin known as to when humans conceived the idea of organizing themselves as a community and later a country, but I believe we still have a lot to learn in terms of justice, fraternity, and society.

I am penning this book to show you the truths of society, regardless of how uncomfortable they are. Over time, I believe the basic elements, such as justice and morality within a society, have been distorted by the people in charge. To prepare for the future, we will have to understand our long-lost history and societal norms. Most importantly, we will have to learn how to balance the two, and that is exactly what this book has to offer. In human history, the notion of religion has always been a profound narrative, providing guidance and purpose to countless lives. One of the earliest edicts bestowed upon humanity, religion offered a framework to shape individuals into better, more virtuous beings. It sought to illuminate the path to righteousness, compassion, and a harmonious existence.

However, the pages of time have witnessed a transformation in the role of religion. Instead of serving as a unifying force, it has, regrettably, become a tool wielded against each other. In the contemporary world, religious differences are frequently exploited, sowing seeds of discord and disharmony not only within specific regions like the sub-continent but also resonating globally.

This transformation prompts a poignant reflection on the essence of religion. What was intended to foster unity, understanding, and a shared sense of purpose has, in some instances, devolved into a source of division and conflict. Yet, amid the prevailing chaos, this book aims to offer readers a profound insight into humanity.

This book reflects the true essence of what it means to be human. It delves into the core values that transcend religious boundaries—values such as compassion, empathy, and a commitment to the well-being of all.

The narrative within these pages unfolds as a testament to the shared humanity that unites us all, irrespective of our diverse faiths and beliefs. Through my words, I hope to kindle a spark within each reader, inspiring them to embrace a more peaceful and prosperous life, look beyond the divisive interpretations of religion, and rediscover the common threads that bind us together as one human family.

I hope my writing can be a reminder that the principles embedded in our shared humanity are the key to unlocking a future marked by unity, compassion, and prosperity. May this book serve as a guiding light, leading readers toward a more enlightened and harmonious existence where the true spirit of humanity prevails.

Chapter 1: Historical Foundations of Indian Society

India, positioned prominently in South Asia, draws its name from the illustrious Indus River. Concerning its cultural and historical roots, the Indian constitution venerates the nation as *Bharata*, paying homage to the legendary figure of Emperor Bharata from the epic *Mahabharata.*

The *Puranas*, ancient scriptures penned in the 5th century CE, narrate tales of Emperor Bharata's valor and leadership. It is believed that under his reign, he unified the diverse regions of the vast subcontinent, ushering in a golden era of peace and prosperity. This epoch of tranquility led to the moniker *Bharatavarsha*, signifying **the realm of Bharata**.

Beyond its historical significance, the Indian subcontinent holds archaeological marvels that bear testimony to its ancient past. With traces of human activity spanning over an astonishing 250,000 years, this region stands as a testament to the resilience and evolution of mankind.

Its landscapes have witnessed the rise and fall of civilizations, the birth of philosophies, and the intermingling of diverse cultures, making it not just a geographical entity but a crucible of human history and innovation.

India, with its intricate tapestry of culture and history, stands as a testament to human evolution in various spheres of life. Beyond its awe-inspiring past, India has been the cradle of profound spiritual and philosophical movements that have shaped the spiritual landscape of the world. The birth and evolution of Hinduism, Jainism, Buddhism, and Sikhism from this ancient land have provided spiritual solace and philosophical insights to countless souls across generations.

Besides a rich cultural and historical past, India is also the birthplace of four great world religions - **Hinduism**, **Jainism**, **Buddhism**, and **Sikhism** - as well as the philosophical school of *Charvaka,* which influenced the development of scientific thought and inquiry. The inventions and innovations of the people of ancient India include many aspects of modern life taken for granted today, including the flush toilet, drainage and sewer systems, public pools, mathematics, veterinary science, plastic surgery, board games, yoga, and meditation, as well as many more.

However, India's legacy isn't confined to the realms of philosophy and spirituality alone. Its ancient scholars and thinkers were pioneers in various fields, manifesting their innovative spirit in myriad ways that still resonate in our daily lives.

India's numerous contributions to spirituality, philosophy, science, and daily life underscore a civilization's relentless pursuit of knowledge and innovation, leaving an indelible imprint on the annals of human history.

In the 19th century, European scholars, while reconstructing early Indian history, often portrayed it as static, emphasizing its spiritual dimensions. German scholar Max Muller leaned heavily on *Sanskritic* traditions, depicting Indian society as an idyllic agrarian culture that prioritized virtues like introspection, contemplation, and detachment from worldly pursuits. This perspective starkly contrasted with the views of James Mill, a Scottish historian and economist. Mill critiqued Indian civilization, deeming it irrational and hindering human progress. He pioneered a classification of Indian history into distinct Hindu, Muslim, and British epochs—a framework that, while historically entrenched, has since been subject to debate and reinterpretation.

Around the 3rd millennium BCE, the **Indus Valley civilization** emerged in present-day Pakistan and parts of north-west India, contemporaneous with other ancient civilizations like **Mesopotamia** and **Ancient Egypt.** Renowned for its meticulously planned urban centers, this civilization stands as one of humanity's earliest, well-organized societies.

However, by the mid-2nd millennium BCE, the once-flourishing Indus Valley civilization waned. Subsequently, the *Aryans*, a group speaking an Indo-European language, migrated from Central Asia into the northern realms of India. Initially arriving as semi-nomadic pastoral groups led by military commanders, they gradually integrated with the indigenous *Dravidian* communities, establishing dominion and forming tribal polities.

The end of the Indus Valley Civilization marked the beginning of the *Vedic* Period, a pivotal era in India's history marked by profound cultural, religious, and social transformations. It was a foundational period where many pillars of traditional Indian culture took shape, including the emergence of Hinduism as a predominant faith and the intricate socio-religious construct of the caste system. Central to this period were the *Vedas*, the revered religious texts that provided spiritual guidance and laid the foundation for societal norms and structures. As society evolved during the *Vedic* Period, a structured social hierarchy, known as the **caste system** or ***Varnas***, began to take shape. Initially, these Varnas might have been distinct categories based on one's occupation and skills.

The *Brahmanas*, occupying the zenith of this hierarchy, were revered as priests and scholars entrusted with the sacred task of preserving and disseminating knowledge. The *Kshatriyas*, the warrior class, held the responsibility of protecting the realm and upholding justice. The *Vaishyas*, predominantly farmers and merchants, played a vital role in sustaining the economy and trade networks. Below them were the *Shudras*, who primarily engaged in labor-intensive tasks, supporting the functioning of society.

However, alongside these primary Varnas existed a marginalized group, the '*Dalits*' or 'untouchables.' Engaged in occupations considered ritually impure, such as handling meat and waste, they faced systemic discrimination and were often ostracized from mainstream society. The precise origins and existence of the *Dalits* during antiquity remain subjects of scholarly debate, with interpretations varying across historical and sociological perspectives.

Over time, the caste system transformed, becoming more ossified. Birth, rather than merit or occupation, became the predominant determinant of one's caste, restricting social mobility and perpetuating entrenched inequalities. Inter-caste marriages were taboo, further reinforcing the boundaries between different *Varnas*.

This rigid interpretation of the caste system was underpinned by the belief in a divine cosmic order, where each caste had a designated role ordained by the supreme deity. The societal structure was perceived as a reflection of this divine order, emphasizing the interdependence of the *Varnas* and their collective responsibility toward maintaining harmony and *Dharma* (righteousness) in the universe.

Therefore, the evolution of the caste system during the *Vedic* Period reflects the intricate interplay between religious beliefs, societal norms, and the quest for cosmic order, leaving an enduring legacy that continues to influence India's socio-cultural realm.

During the *Vedic* Period, while the spiritual beliefs that would later define the era were believed to have ancient roots, it was this era that witnessed their formalization into what is now recognized as 'Sanatan Dharma,' or the 'Eternal Order.' This tradition eventually evolved into what the world recognizes today as **Hinduism**. Interestingly, the term 'Hinduism' is believed to have its etymological origins in the name of the Indus (or Sindus) River, where adherents frequently congregated, leading to the term 'Sindus' and eventually 'Hindus.'

Central to the philosophy of *Sanatan Dharma* is the conviction that the cosmos, as well as human existence, follow a predetermined order imbued with purpose. Embracing and aligning oneself with this cosmic order is perceived as the pathway to leading a fulfilled life in harmony with the design of the universe. While some might perceive the Sanatan Dharma as a polytheistic faith due to its diverse nature, it fundamentally upholds monotheistic principles. At its core lies the belief in

Brahman, the supreme cosmic entity encompassing the Self, the universe, and the architect behind its creation. Given the ineffable magnitude of *Brahman*, comprehending this entity directly proves elusive, leading to the manifestation of various deities within the Hindu pantheon as accessible facets of *Brahman*.

It is believed that *Brahman* established and sustained the universe's inherent order. This profound notion of cosmic harmony mirrored the societal cohesion and stability witnessed during the *Vedic* era, marked by centralized governance and the seamless integration of cultural norms into daily life. It also birthed seminal religious and literary masterpieces, including the *Vedas*, the *Puranas*, the *Mahabharata* (an epic poem), the *Bhagavad Gita*, and the *Ramayana* (an epic poem), which continue to resonate profoundly within Hindu philosophy and culture.

In the 6th century BCE, a transformative period in religious thought witnessed the emergence of two profound reformers: **Vardhamana Mahavira** (c. 599-527 BCE) and **Siddhartha Gautama** (c. 563 to c. 483 BCE). Both thinkers diverged from the established tenets of *Sanatan Dharma* to establish the distinct faiths of **Jainism** and **Buddhism**, respectively.

This religious evolution was emblematic of broader societal and cultural shifts, marked by the emergence of autonomous city-states, the ascent of formidable kingdoms like the **Magadha Kingdom** under **Bimbisara's** reign, and a surge in philosophical inquiries that questioned traditional Hindu orthodoxy. *Mahavira*, in his teachings, distanced himself from the authority of the *Vedas*, emphasizing personal accountability for attaining salvation and enlightenment—a sentiment later echoed by **Buddha**. Concurrently, the *Charvaka* philosophical tradition presented a radical departure from conventional religious paradigms. It eschewed supernatural constructs, advocating instead for a worldview grounded solely in sensory perception. The *Charvaka* philosophy prioritized hedonism, asserting that life's ultimate pursuit should be personal pleasure and gratification.

While the Charvaka school's prominence was depleted over time, its legacy was instrumental in developing a pragmatic intellectual milieu. This evolving mindset laid the groundwork for an emphasis on empirical observation and methodical inquiry, setting the stage for the future interplay between religion, philosophy, and empirical science.

In 330 BCE, the Persian grip on northern India was supplanted by the ambitious campaign of Alexander the Great, who ventured into the subcontinent following Persia's decline. This incursion ushered in a period of Greco-Buddhist cultural fusion, profoundly influencing northern India's artistic, religious, and sartorial landscapes. Notably, artworks of this age belonged to the Gandhara School of Art, depicting Buddha and other revered figures in distinctly Hellenic garb and postures.

Post-Alexander, the **Mauryan Empire**, headed by **Chandragupta Maurya** (r. c. 321-297 BCE), ascended to prominence. By the end of the 3rd century BCE, this empire held sway over a vast expanse of northern India. Chandragupta's successor, **Bindusara** (r. 298-272 BCE), further expanded the empire's territorial reach, encompassing nearly the entirety of the Indian subcontinent.

The Mauryan grandeur was at its prime under the illustrious reign of **Ashoka the Great** (r. 268-232 BCE). His transformative journey began with the conquest of the Kalinga region, a campaign marred by immense bloodshed, with casualties exceeding 100,000. Deeply perturbed by the aftermath of this conquest, Ashoka underwent a profound spiritual metamorphosis, embracing the principles of Buddhism wholeheartedly.

Under Ashoka's patronage, Buddhism experienced a renaissance. He fostered the establishment of numerous monastic institutions, bestowed generous endowments upon Buddhist congregations, and commissioned an impressive array of stupas—estimated at 84,000—to venerate Buddha's teachings. In a significant act of reverence, Ashoka designated Lumbini, traditionally regarded as Buddha's birthplace, by erecting a commemorative pillar and promulgating the iconic Edicts of Ashoka. These edicts served as beacons, championing Buddhist ethics and values.

Before Ashoka's transformative reign, Buddhism, though profound, remained a nascent faith seeking broader acceptance. However, Ashoka's missionary endeavors, spreading Buddhist tenets beyond the subcontinent's borders, catalyzed its ascension, transforming Buddhism into a global spiritual force.

During this period, the *Vyasa* (transl. compiler or the one who classified the scriptures) compiled the influential *Puranas*, shaping the narrative and essence of Hindu mythology. Meanwhile, the iconic *Ajanta* and *Ellora* caves began to take form, showcasing intricate carvings and expansive vaulted chambers that stand as testaments to ancient artistry. The literary realm flourished with luminaries like *Kalidasa*, who penned the timeless classic *Shakuntala*. Concurrently,

Vatsyayana either composed or synthesized the *Kamasutra*, a treatise on love and life.

Despite the foundational influence of traditional Hindu ideologies, the visionary rulers of the **Gupta Empire**, in a departure from convention, championed **Buddhism** as the state religion. This deliberate patronage explains the profusion of Buddhist artistic creations, eclipsing Hindu artworks prominently showcased in sites like *Ajanta* and *Ellora*. The empire experienced a gradual decline, marked by a series of ineffectual rulers, ultimately culminating in its dissolution around 550 CE. Stepping into this power vacuum was **Harshavardhana** (590-647 CE), who governed the realm for an impressive span of 42 years. Beyond his political acumen, Harsha was a literary luminary, having authored three plays and various other literary works. A fervent patron of the arts, he ardently upheld Buddhist principles, notably prohibiting animal slaughter within his dominion, although he recognized the inevitability of human casualties in warfare.

Renowned for his military prowess, Harsha faced defeat in battle only once throughout his illustrious life. Under his stewardship, northern India experienced a renaissance. However, with his demise, the political landscape unraveled. Despite the Guptas and, subsequently, Harshavardhana successfully fending off *Hun* invasions, the region descended into turmoil post-Harsha's rule, splintering into fragmented kingdoms devoid of the cohesion needed to thwart external aggressors.

In 712 CE (Common Era), the Muslim commander **Muhammed bin Qasim** seized control of northern India, consolidating his influence in present-day Pakistan. This conquest marked the eclipse of native Indian empires, ushering in an era dominated by autonomous city-states or communities governed by urban centers.

The Islamic Sultanates emerged in what is now Pakistan, gradually expanding toward the northwest. The divergent religious philosophies vying for prominence in the region, coupled with linguistic diversity, posed challenges to fostering the unified cultural and intellectual flourishing reminiscent of the Gupta era. This fragmentation rendered the territory susceptible to the expansive reach of the Islamic Mughal Empire. Subsequently, India became a crucible of varied foreign dominions, including the Portuguese, French, and British, enduring external influences until eventually reclaiming sovereignty in 1947. Throughout its millennia-long journey, India stands as a captivating mosaic of cultures, traditions, and civilizations, each layer adding depth to its multifaceted identity. From the sophisticated urban planning of the ancient Indus Valley Civilization to the philosophical profundity of the Vedic Period, and from the grandeur of the Mauryan and Gupta empires to the artistic splendors of the Mughal era, India's narrative is replete with innovation, enlightenment, and transformation.

Its landscapes have echoed the footsteps of countless dynasties, scholars, traders, and explorers, each contributing to its ever-evolving history and tradition. The rhythmic chants of Vedic hymns, the intricate carvings of Ajanta and Ellora, the majestic forts and palaces, and the vibrant festivals —all bear testament to a diverse Indian civilization. India's history is not merely a chronicle of kings and battles but a saga of ideas, philosophies, and innovations that have shaped the course of human civilization.

As we reflect upon India's legacy, we are reminded of its enduring spirit—a confluence of the ancient and the modern, the traditional and the contemporary. It serves as a poignant reminder of the interconnectedness of human civilizations and the boundless potential of a nation whose soulful journey continues to inspire and resonate across the annals of time.

Chapter 2: The Arrival and Establishment of Islam

With a population exceeding 500 million, the Indian subcontinent, comprising India, Pakistan, and Bangladesh, stood as one of the most significant Muslim population hubs globally. Since the inception of Islam in India, its influence has profoundly shaped the region and its inhabitants.

Various hypotheses attempt to explain the widespread presence of Muslims in India today. Politically motivated factions, like the *Hindutva* movement in India, sometimes depict Islam as an alien presence, attributing its spread solely to Arab and Persian invasions. However, the historical reality offers a rather multifaceted narrative.

When considering South Asia, images of majestic forts, intricate miniature paintings, grand tombs, lush gardens, and iconic structures like the Taj Mahal often come to mind. These landmarks stand as testaments to the opulence and cultural refinement of the Mughal Empire (1526-1857). Under its reign, a unique aristocratic culture flourished, marked by remarkable achievements in arts, music, poetry, courtly manners, ceremonial practices, and imperial artifacts.

The **Mughal Empire** stands out as one of the most centralized states of the early modern era, commanding vast territories and a sizable population. By the end of the 17th century, the Mughal emperors held sway over an estimated 100-150 million people and controlled approximately 3.2 million square kilometers (about 1.23 million square miles) of the Indian subcontinent.[1] Their dominion stretched across regions encompassing present-day India, Pakistan, Bangladesh, and even parts of Afghanistan, including areas like Kabul, Kashmir, Delhi, Bengal, Odisha, Gujarat, Rajasthan, and sections of the Deccan.

The era of the victors of the First Battle of Panipat (1526) coincided with significant global developments. As historian John Richards elucidates, this era witnessed the integration of global maritime routes, a boom in the textile industry, demographic expansions, and the diffusion of technology. The Mughals built upon the administrative and cultural foundations laid by preceding dynasties, enabling the expansive empire to thrive.

It's noteworthy that Islam's roots in South Asia predate the Mughal era by nearly a millennium. Islam first permeated the region in the 7th century when it was introduced by Arab traders along the Malabar Sea coasts of southern India and Sri Lanka.

These traders, often endorsed by non-Muslim monarchs, played a pivotal role in fostering economic ties between South Asia and Southwest Asia. Subsequently, during the Umayyad caliphate based in Damascus in the 8th century CE, Arabic-speaking Muslim merchants ventured into Sindh, now a province in Pakistan.

Over time, the Muslim community in South Asia grew, facilitated by intermarriages and conversions, spanning both pre-Mughal and Mughal periods. These endeavors bore fruit,

---

[1] https://www.asianstudies.org/publications/eaa/archives/islam-and-the-mughal-empire-in-south-asia-1526-1857/

connecting Islam to the broader Indian societal framework. As is characteristic of many religious missionary movements, trade and commerce played a concurrent role with religious propagation. The pre-existing presence of Arabs in India before Muhammad's era likely facilitated the spread of Islam. This was further enhanced as Arab traders, who were already established in India, embraced Islam, leveraging their established networks in India's richly diverse religious and cultural milieu.

The rise of Islam in South Asia coincided with the Turko-Muslim invasions during medieval times, encompassing regions that now constitute Pakistan and parts of modern-day India. These rulers assumed administrative control over extensive territories in India. Since its inception in the region, Islam has enriched Indian history through its profound religious, artistic, philosophical, cultural, social, and political contributions.

The Islamic footprint in South Asia predates the Muslim invasions. The initial influence began in the early 7th century with Arab traders, who frequented the Malabar region, connecting it to Southeast Asian ports even before Islam took root in Arabia. As Islam emerged, Arabs emerged as significant cultural influencers. Arab merchants disseminated the faith during their travels, with Malik Bin Deenar erecting the first Indian mosque in Kodungallur in 612 C.E. on the request of Cheraman Perumal during the lifetime of Prophet Muhammad(PBUH).

The first great expansion of Islam into India came during the Umayyad Dynasty of caliphs, who were based in Damascus. In 711, the Umayyads appointed Muhammad Bin Qasim (who was only 17 at the time) from *Ta'if* to extend Umayyad control into Sindh. Sindh is the land around the Indus River in the

Northwestern part of the subcontinent in present-day Pakistan. Muhammad bin Qasim led his army of 6,000 soldiers to the far eastern reaches of Persia and Makran. He encountered little resistance as he made his way into India. When he reached the city of Nerun, on the banks of the Indus River, he was welcomed into the city by the Buddhist monks who controlled it. Most cities along the Indus thus voluntarily came under Muslim control, with no fighting. In some cases, oppressed Buddhist minorities reached out to the Muslim armies for protection against Hindu governors.

Despite the support and approval of much of the population, the Raja of Sindh, Dahir, opposed the Muslim expansion and mobilized his army against Muhammad bin Qasim. In 712, the two armies met, with a decisive victory for the Muslims. With the victory, all of Sindh came under Muslim control.

It is important to note, however, that the population of Sindh was not forced to convert to Islam at all. There was no change in day-to-day life for almost everyone. Muhammad bin Qasim promised security and religious freedom to all Hindus and Buddhists under his control.

For instance, the Brahman caste continued their jobs as tax collectors, and Buddhist monks continued to maintain their monasteries. Due to his religious tolerance and justice, many cities regularly greeted him and his armies with dancing and music.

Meanwhile, in the Malabar region (known as Bombay's coastal region today), the Mappilas likely constituted the earliest Muslim converts. The coast witnessed fervent missionary activities, leading to a significant number of locals embracing Islam and assimilating into the Mappila community, comprising both Arab lineage and indigenous converts. By the 8th century, under Muhammad bin Qasim, Syrian Arabs had conquered Sindh, marking it as the eastern frontier of the **Umayyad Caliphate**. Subsequently, Mahmud of Ghazni, in the 10th century, incorporated Punjab into the **Ghaznavid Empire**, launching several incursions into India. The culmination came in the late 12th century with Muhammad of Ghor's conquest, establishing the Delhi Sultanate.

Not to mention this era was also marked by the spread of *Sufism* (a mystic body of religious practice found within Islam that is characterized by a focus on Islamic purification, spirituality, ritualism, asceticism, and esotericism).

Followers of *Sufism* exerted a significant influence on the dissemination of Islam throughout India. Their success in this endeavor can be attributed to the resonance between *Sufi* principles and certain aspects of Indian philosophical thought, notably nonviolence and monism.

The *Sufis'* flexible and inclusive interpretation of Islam facilitated a more receptive environment for Hindus. Eminent figures such as **Hazrat Khawaja Muin-ud-din Chisti, Nizam-ud-din Auliya, Shah Jalal, Amir Khusro, Sarkar Sabir Pak**, and **Waris Pak** nurtured a cadre of *Sufis* dedicated to advancing Islam across various Indian regions.

In the context of the established Islamic rule in India, *Sufis* infused vibrance and cultural richness, tempering what might otherwise have been austere administrations. Notably, the Sufi movement resonated deeply with marginalized communities, including artisans and those considered 'untouchables,' serving as a vital bridge between Islam and indigenous traditions. While historical records indicate instances of forceful conversions by certain Sufi factions, figures like Ahmed Sirhindi of the *Naqshbandi* Sufi order ardently advocated for peaceful conversions, emphasizing mutual respect and understanding. *Sufism*, a mystical dimension within Islam, offers a path distinct from the more legalistic approach of *Sharia*. *Sufis* seek a direct spiritual connection with God, achieving a revered status as a *Pir* or living saint. *Pirs* often guide disciples (*murids*), establishing spiritual lineages that endure across generations.

The thirteenth century saw the rise of *Sufi* orders in India, particularly following **Moinuddin Chishti's** ministry in Ajmer, Rajasthan. Renowned for his spiritual eminence, Chishti attracted numerous converts, with his *Chishtiyya* order emerging as a dominant *Sufi* lineage in India. Concurrently, *Sufi* orders from Central and Southwest Asia also influenced India's Islamic landscape, facilitating the religion's propagation.

The waves of Muslim armies that entered India generally followed a consistent pattern. Notable leaders like **Mahmud of Ghazni** and **Muhammad Tughluq** expanded Muslim territories without significantly altering the existing religious or social structures of Indian society.

Given that pre-Islamic India operated on a strict caste system, conversions to Islam unfolded gradually. At times, entire caste groups would embrace Islam, driven by various motivations. Many were drawn to Islam's principle of equality, contrasting with the rigid hierarchy of the caste system, where one's birth determined societal status and limited social mobility. Embracing Islam offered avenues for upward mobility and emancipation from the constraints of the caste system, particularly the dominance of the Brahmin caste. While Buddhism once flourished in the region, its decline under Muslim rule was not a result of violent suppression. Historically, individuals seeking refuge from the caste system often gravitated toward urban centers and adopted Buddhism. With the advent of Islam as an alternative, many chose to convert to Islam while retaining their caste identities. Claims suggesting a violent eradication of Buddhism under Muslim rule lack substantive evidence. Buddhists generally coexisted peacefully with their Muslim counterparts without instances of forced conversions or persecution.

The propagation of Islam in India was also facilitated by itinerant scholars and teachers. These Muslim scholars traversed the length and breadth of the country, disseminating knowledge about Islam. Many advocated *Sufism*, a mystical dimension of Islam that resonated with diverse audiences. These wandering scholars played a pivotal role in popularizing Islam, reaching not just the elite but also the masses in rural areas.

While certain narratives suggest that the large Muslim population in India is a result of coercive measures and forced conversions, such claims lack substantial evidence. The historical record does not strongly support the notion of widespread forced conversions. While Muslim rulers did supplant Hindu monarchs in various regions, they largely refrained from altering the existing societal structures.

Had Islam been propagated primarily through conquest and violence, one would expect the Muslim populace in India to be predominantly concentrated in regions adjacent to other Islamic civilizations. Yet, we observed a dispersed Muslim presence across the Indian subcontinent. For instance, Bangladesh, with its population of approximately 150 million Muslims, is geographically distant from other Muslim-majority regions, separated by predominantly Hindu territories in India. Similarly, isolated Muslim communities thrive in areas like central India and eastern Sri Lanka. These dispersed Muslim communities underscore the peaceful spread of Islam in India, transcending the presence or absence of Muslim political governance. If forced conversions had been the primary mechanism of Islam's dissemination, the existence of such diverse Muslim communities across the subcontinent would be improbable.

In the 20th century, South Asia's Muslim community witnessed a tumultuous trajectory. After **the 1946 Lahore Resolution**, the Muslim League leaders founded Pakistan as a sovereign Muslim-majority nation after gaining independence from British colonial rule.

Notably, the Muslim populations in both India and Pakistan are roughly equivalent. Distinguished figures like former Indian President **APJ Abdul Kalam**, among others before him, have been Muslims.

Additionally, numerous politicians, sports personalities, and Bollywood celebrities in India also hail from the Muslim community. However, sporadic instances of communal violence have marred relations between Muslim communities and their Hindu, Sikh, and Christian counterparts. The **Muslim Personal Law (Shariat) Application Act** of 1937 prescribes the application of Muslim Personal Law for various aspects of Muslim life in India, including marriage, mahr (dower), divorce, maintenance, gifts, waqf, wills, and inheritance. Generally, courts apply the Hanafi Sunni law, making exceptions only in cases where Shia law significantly diverges from Sunni practices.

While the Indian constitution upholds equal rights for all citizens regardless of their religious affiliations, **Article 44** advocates for a **Uniform Civil Code**. However, efforts by successive governments to implement a common civil code have met with strong opposition from the Muslim community. Many Indian Muslims perceive such initiatives as potential threats to the distinct cultural identity of minority groups within the nation.

India hosts numerous esteemed Muslim educational institutions. These include **Aligarh Muslim University**, which encompasses institutions like the **Deccan College of Engineering**, the **Deccan School of Hospital Management**, and the **Deccan College of Medical Sciences**. Other prominent universities and colleges are **Jamia Millia Islamia**, **Hamdard University**, **Maulana Azad Education Society** in Aurangabad, **Dr. Rafiq Zakariya Campus** in Aurangabad, **Crescent Engineering College**, and **Al-Kabir Educational Society.**

In addition to these, India is home to traditional Islamic universities such as Sunni Markaz in Kerala, which is recognized as the largest charitable Islamic institution in the country. Other notable institutions include **Raza Academy, Al Jamiatul Ashrafia** in Azamgarh, **Dar-ul-Uloom Deoband, and Dar-ul-Uloom Nadwatul Ulama.** The majority of Muslims in India predominantly align with either the Sunni *Deobandi* or Sunni *Barelwi* sects. However, a segment also associates with Shia, Sufi, Salafi, and various smaller sects. Among Islamic seminaries in India, *Dar-ul-Uloom*

Deoband stands out as the most influential, rivaled globally only by Egypt's **Al-Azhar University** in terms of its impact. The conservative Islamic ethos in India finds its educational grounding in the myriad religious training institutes or madrasas across the nation. These institutions emphasize Quranic and Islamic studies in Arabic and Persian. Notably, several national movements have emanated from this conservative Muslim segment. The **Jamaat-e-Islami**, established in 1941, advocates for a distinctly Islamic governance model. Another significant group, the *Tablighi Jamaat*, emerged post-1940s, emphasizing personal spiritual renewal, missionary activities, and adherence to orthodox practices. This group often critiques certain practices associated with Sufi shrines and remains influential among religious leaders. Concurrently, some religious scholars endorse popular religious practices, venerating pirs and the Prophet's legacy.

In a contrasting vein, a secularizing movement championed by Syed Ahmad Khan led to the inception of **Aligarh Muslim University** in 1875, initially as the **Muhammadan Anglo-Oriental College**. Distinguished by its modern curriculum, **Aligarh Muslim University** stands apart from other major Islamic educational institutions in India. The arrival of Islamic rule in India in the late twelfth century AD heralded a transformative phase in Indian architecture as well. Islamic influences introduced novel elements such as geometric shapes, intricate calligraphic inscriptions, and decorative techniques using colored marble, painted plaster, and vibrant glazed tiles.

Diverging from the traditional Indian trabeated architectural style, which relies on horizontal beams, Islamic architecture favored the arcuate approach, employing arches and domes. While the foundational concepts of arches and domes predated Islamic influence, it was the Muslim architects who refined and popularized these features in India. Additionally, they introduced the use of mortar as a binding agent in construction, enhancing structural integrity. Leveraging scientific principles from various civilizations, they innovated building techniques that not only bolstered strength but also offered architects greater design flexibility.

Before its introduction in India, Islamic architectural styles evolved through various iterations in regions like Egypt, Iran, and Iraq. However, in India, these designs predominantly manifested as mortar-masonry constructions using finely dressed stones, diverging from the brick and plaster predominant elsewhere. The profound expertise of Indian craftsmen, honed over centuries, seamlessly merged with Islamic architectural concepts, giving rise to the distinctive Indo-Islamic architectural style.

In India, Islamic architecture can be broadly categorized into religious and secular forms. Religious structures encompass mosques and tombs, while palaces and forts exemplify the secular facet. Forts, in particular, were meticulously designed, featuring not only defensive structures but also self-contained townships, illustrating a harmonious blend of functionality and aesthetics.

The mosque, or masjid, embodies the essence of Islamic art in its most elemental form. Typically, a mosque features an open courtyard encircled by a pillared verandah crowned with a dome. A mihrab, indicating the direction of the qibla, serves as the focal point for prayers. Adjacent to the mihrab, the *mimbar* or pulpit stands, from which the Imam leads the congregation. A defining feature of mosques is the minaret, an elevated platform from which the call to prayer resonates. Larger congregational mosques, known as Jama Masjids, are central to community gatherings, especially for Friday prayers. Conversely, the tomb, or *maqbara,* introduced a distinct architectural paradigm. While mosques emphasize simplicity, tombs, ranging from modest graves like Aurangzeb's to grand edifices like the Taj Mahal, epitomize architectural grandeur. Typically, a tomb comprises a central chamber or *huzzah*, housing the cenotaph or *zarih* beneath an ornate dome. Beneath this lies the actual burial chamber or maqbara. While smaller tombs might feature a mihrab, larger mausoleums often include a separate mosque. Surrounding the entire tomb complex, or *rauza*, is an enclosing wall. A dargah denotes the resting place of a revered Muslim saint. Intricate Quranic inscriptions adorn the walls, ceilings, pillars, and domes of these structures.

Islamic architectural evolution in India can be categorized into three distinct styles: the Delhi or Imperial style (1191 to 1557 C.E.), characterized by its early architectural expressions; the Provincial style, encompassing regions like Jaunpur and the Deccan, showcasing regional influences; and the Mughal style (1526 to 1707 C.E.), epitomized by its grandeur and synthesis of diverse architectural elements.

Islam in India navigated the intricate landscape of coexistence with several indigenous religions. Given that Hinduism, Jainism, and Buddhism originated in India, Islam's interactions were marked by mutual influence and accommodation.

Even as Buddhism waned in India from the eighth century C.E., it retained significant influence. Islam's engagement with a diverse array of religions—including Hinduism, Jainism, Buddhism, Judaism, and Christianity—presented challenges, especially during India's transition to independence from British colonial rule. A significant segment of India's Muslim populace resonated with the vision of leaders like **Muhammad Ali Jinnah**, **Nawab Liaquat Ali Khan**, and **Huseyn Shaheed Suhrawardy**, advocating for a separate nation. Many Muslims believed that harmonious coexistence with the predominant Hindu majority might compromise their religious identity.

This sentiment culminated in the establishment of Pakistan in 1947 and, later, Bangladesh in 1971. Meanwhile, the Muslim community remaining in India has endeavored, with varying degrees of success, to foster cooperation within the diverse religious mosaic of the nation.

Islam holds a significant place in India. Given the Indian subcontinent's current status as a diverse region characterized by various ethnicities and religions, it becomes crucial to recognize the genuine role Islam has played and continues to play. Assertions that paint Islam as an invasive faith in India are not only historically inaccurate but also misrepresent the peaceful manner in which Islam harmoniously integrated and spread across the Indian landscape.

Chapter 3: The British Era and Partition

The Mughals established a formidable empire that stood as a pinnacle of influence in Indian history and culture. With over two centuries of successful governance over a significant portion of India, the dynasty distinguished itself through capable rulers and a well-organized administrative structure.

History proved beyond a doubt that every empire that evolved and flourished across centuries dug its own grave. Every other historian since the 18th century has debated the causes of the decline of the Mughal Empire. The notion of decline envisages a prior state of perfection, efflorescence, harmony, and cohesion, in contrast to corruption, moral degradation, and loss of ethical values, principles, and customs.

The Mughal emperors actively championed the realms of art and learning, leaving an indelible mark on these cultural spheres. Notably, Mughal architecture gained widespread acclaim for its aesthetic harmony and beauty. Nevertheless, numerous factors ultimately contributed to the decline and fall of the dynasty.

Initially, Mughal emperors were recognized for their adept approach to integrating the diverse peoples they conquered into their government and military, fostering a sense of inclusivity. However, in the later years of the empire, a shift toward autocracy and intolerance emerged. Hindus and other groups were marginalized, deemed inferior, and faced exclusion from the Mughal court along with heavy taxation. The rise of religious intolerance destroyed Hindu and Sikh temples and schools. These policies fueled widespread discontent and uprisings against the

Mughals, leading to the fragmentation of their kingdom and a significant weakening of their rule. Under Aurangzeb's rule (1658–1707), the Mughal Empire experienced a notable economic downturn. The imposition of high taxes by the emperor left the farming population in a state of impoverishment.

Concurrently, there was a gradual deterioration in the quality of Mughal governance. Subsequent emperors displayed limited interest in administration and reluctance to invest in agriculture, technology, or the military. In some instances, emperors actively discouraged economic prosperity, harboring concerns that a prosperous elite might amass independent military forces. This environment eventually led to local leaders rebelling and asserting their independence from the central government, expediting the decline of the empire.

At its zenith, the Mughal Empire extended across most of Afghanistan and the Indian subcontinent. However, by the time Muhammad Shah ascended the throne in 1719, the empire was already undergoing fragmentation.

Dynastic conflicts, factional rivalries, and the disruptive invasion of northern India by the Iranian conqueror Nadir Shah in 1739 expedited this process. Following Muhammad Shah's death in 1748, the Marathas effectively took control of the majority of northern India, leaving the Mughal rule confined to a limited area around Delhi. Subsequently, the British asserted their control over this region in 1803. By the mid-1800s, the Mughal Empire had ceded all its territory to rivals and the British, marking the conclusion of its once expansive influence. Established in 1600 (under a Royal Charter created on 31st December 1600), the British East India Company initially focused on trade with the

Mughal Empire. However, with the gradual weakening of the empire, the British increased their influence over Mughal rulers.

With a massive private army and the backing of the British government, the EIC looted the Indian subcontinent until anarchy necessitated that the government step in and take over EIC possessions in 1858.

In 1757, British forces emerged victorious in the Battle of Plassey, defeating the Nawab (ruler) of Bengal and French forces. This triumph marked a turning point as the East India Company assumed political control over a significant portion of the Indian subcontinent.

Although Mughal emperors retained nominal thrones, their actual authority dwindled. Bahadur Shah Zafar governed a diminished Mughal Empire largely confined to Delhi's Red Fort, devoid of substantial influence across the broader Indian landscape.

Following the Indian Rebellion of 1857, the British Administration expelled him from Delhi, transporting him to a prison in Rangoon, Burma, where he ultimately passed away, thereby underscoring the culmination of British dominance in the region.

The East India Company (EIC) served as the instrument through which Britain pursued its imperialistic agenda in Asia, amassing considerable wealth through its expansive trade network involving spices, tea, textiles, and opium. It faced criticism for its monopolistic practices, onerous trading terms, corrupt dealings, and detrimental impact on the wool trade. Beyond economic concerns, the EIC forcefully displaced rulers, exploited resources and suppressed cultural traditions within its extensive territories. The company's directors and shareholders amassed enormous fortunes, while India, in stark contrast, experienced increasing impoverishment. Evolving beyond a mere trading entity, the EIC transformed into a quasi-state, an empire within an empire, with accountability restricted solely to its shareholders.

British rule in India introduced religious and political rifts, fostering heightened animosity within communities and culminating in the partition of India in 1947. Imperial strategies like **divide and rule** exacerbated tensions between different groups, underscoring the divisive impact imposed by the colonizers to a significant degree. Not to mention, the distinctive characteristic of colonial India was how imperial social changes and policies generated the initial tensions between Hindus and Muslims.

In the mid-nineteenth century, scholars delved deeply into the effects of colonialism on the Hindu-Muslim dynamic, both before and after India gained independence. The conventional interpretation posits that the colonial history of India played a pivotal role in acknowledging Muslim identities, ultimately leading to the partition of British India in 1947. This represented a significant manifestation of the potent intersection between religious narratives and political movements. India's colonial framework fueled the animosity between Hindus and Muslims. The minority status of Muslims in British India undoubtedly played a role, prompting this community to establish a distinct political identity distinct from British and Hindu influences. The partition further heightened state fragmentation, intensifying over subsequent years. Recognizing the significance of India's colonial history is essential for comprehending the gradual strengthening of Muslim consciousness. Until the mid-1940s, Hindus, Muslims, Sikhs, Jains, Buddhists, Christians, Parsis, Jews, and others peacefully coexisted for centuries across various regions in South Asia. The pre-partition populations reflected a more cosmopolitan makeup. Religion was primarily practiced at home, with major festivals like Diwali, Eid, and Christmas being universally celebrated, and for the majority, religion was not a defining factor for identification.

However, around 1945, as World War II concluded and the British prepared to depart from their Indian territories, political groups advocating distinct nationhood ideologies gained momentum.

Notions of a Muslim-majority Pakistan, a Sikh Khalistan, and a secular versus Hindu India began to take root in local politics. The shift marked by isolated incidents of violence—shootings, stabbings, and massacres based on religion—started making headlines, spreading fear, distrust, and anger.

Oral histories indicate that these initial events were typically orchestrated by fanatical individuals or groups aligned with right-wing religious ideologies.

Over time, the amalgamation of religion and politics resulted in religious ideologues gaining representation within local political parties.

In colonial India, religious identities started to crystallize within political factions, escalating challenges for Hindus and Muslims. The predominant hurdle confronting India during this period was religious conflict, underscored by the persistent rivalry between the two principal political entities of the time:

the Indian Congress Party (INC) and the All-India Muslim League (Muslim League). Each of these parties grappled with the opposing ideologies of the other, culminating in the partition of British India into two independent states—India and Pakistan.

The attainment of India's independence and the emergence of Pakistan in 1947 undeniably exerted a profound influence on Hindu-Muslim relations, marked by persistent religious tension and a rise in community riots.

The Partition resulted in substantial loss of life and livelihoods and had profound repercussions on education and economies in South Asia, impacts that persist to this day, as suggested by our research. While certain aspects of this period remain inadequately explored, the undeniable consequences cannot be overlooked. The enduring mass trauma, revealed through new findings on post-traumatic stress disorder science and epigenetic inheritance, continues to affect millions in the modern generation.

Despite enduring violent times, a significant majority of the 8,000 individuals we have interviewed do not harbor resentments toward those belonging to religious groups that were hostile toward them in 1947. However, subsequent generations seem to harbor stronger and more nationalistic sentiments toward "the other side," a sentiment not experienced during their upbringing.

This shift is due to Partition witnesses possessing pre-Partition memories of harmonious coexistence with "the other," while only memories of violence and regret associated with Partition, which are more vivid, are selectively passed down to the next generation. These memories, coupled with nationalistic rhetoric during India and Pakistan's nation-building efforts and one-sided knowledge of ongoing conflicts between the two nations, contribute to a heightened bias in subsequent generations.

A deeper and clearer understanding of the origins of Partition violence can play a constructive role in addressing contemporary social issues rooted in one-sided histories of interfaith relationships from that period.

It is crucial to draw lessons from the communal violence and radicalization during the Partition era before it escalates into chaos once again. History has shown us the repercussions of such events, and it is imperative to learn from them.

We have a choice between imparting teachings of tolerance, acceptance, and understanding or promoting intolerance and hatred toward those different from ourselves. As the global population expands, our children and grandchildren will encounter increasing diversity. Starting now, we can educate them on how to respond in more constructive and inclusive ways.

Chapter 4: Post-independence India

Secularism in India, characterized by distinct differences from the Western model, remains a contentious subject within the country. Advocates of the Indian approach argue that it upholds the values of "minority rights and pluralism."

Detractors, however, label the Indian form as "pseudo-secularism." Those in favor contend that the implementation of a uniform civil code, ensuring equal laws for all citizens regardless of their religious affiliation, could potentially impose majority Hindu perspectives and principles. Critics counter that India's acknowledgment of certain religious laws undermines the foundational principle of equality before the law.

Since gaining independence in 1947, India has functioned as a secular state, with these secular principles codified in its constitution. Jawaharlal Nehru, India's inaugural prime minister, and B.R. Ambedkar, the law minister, are acknowledged as pivotal figures in shaping the nation's contemporary history and fostering its commitment to secular values.

The 42nd Amendment of the Constitution of India, implemented in 1976, officially proclaimed India as a secular nation in the Preamble. However, the 1994 S. R. Bommai v. Union of India case, heard by the Supreme Court of India, affirmed that India had been secular since the inception of the republic.

The court's ruling underscored the clear separation between the state and religion, stating, "In matters of State, religion has no place. Any State government pursuing non-secular policies or actions contravenes the constitutional mandate and subjects itself to action under Article 356." Additionally, constitutionally, state-owned educational institutions are barred from providing religious instructions, and Article 27 prohibits the use of taxpayers' money for the promotion of any specific religion.

Formally, secularism has consistently served as a guiding principle for modern India. However, the Indian approach to secularism doesn't entirely segregate religion and state. The Indian Constitution permits substantial state intervention in religious matters, evident in actions like the constitutional abolition of untouchability and the opening of all Hindu temples to individuals from 'lower castes.' The extent of separation between the state and religion has fluctuated with various court decisions and executive orders since the Republic's inception.

In the realm of law in contemporary India, personal laws governing aspects such as marriage, divorce, inheritance, and alimony differ based on one's religious affiliation, with Muslims having the option to marry under secular law if they choose.

The Indian Constitution also allows for partial financial support to religious schools and state financing of religious buildings and infrastructure.

The federal and state governments administer and fund the Islamic Central Wakf Council and several Hindu temples of significant religious importance through the Places of Worship (Special Provisions) Act, 1991, and the Ancient Monuments and Archaeological Sites and Remains Act, 1958. These acts mandate state maintenance of religious structures established before August 15, 1947, while preserving their religious character. Efforts to accommodate religious laws in India have given rise to various challenges, including debates over the acceptability of practices such as polygamy, unequal inheritance rights, unilateral divorce rights favoring certain males, and conflicting interpretations of religious texts.

Following independence, India confronted a myriad of challenges, encompassing economic instability, social divides, and political upheaval. A primary hurdle was the reconstruction of an economy ravaged by British colonial rule.

India grappled with entrenched social inequalities stemming from its caste system, alongside religious tensions among Hindus, Muslims, and other communities. Addressing these disparities involved initiatives like affirmative action through reservation policies and social welfare programs.

Mentioned below are some of the challenges faced by the people at the time:

•   **Communal Violence:** The period of Partition was marred by widespread communal violence, creating not only a division of assets but also triggering a significant refugee crisis. This turbulent time set the stage for the longstanding Kashmir problem.

•   **Mass Poverty:** At the dawn of Independence, India grappled with extensive poverty, affecting approximately 80% or around 250 million people. Famine and hunger necessitated external assistance to ensure food security.

•   **Illiteracy:** In 1947, with a population of about 340 million, India faced a literacy rate of merely 12%, encompassing around 41 million people.

- **Low Economic Capacity:** The economic challenges included stagnant agriculture and a limited industrial base. In 1947, agriculture contributed to 54% of India's GDP, with 60% of the population relying on it for livelihood. The centrally planned economy phase from the 1950s to 1980s saw a modest annual growth rate of 3.5% (known as the Hindu rate of growth), while per capita income growth averaged 1.3%.

- **Linguistic Reorganization:** The arbitrary boundaries of British Indian provinces, lacking cultural and linguistic coherence, led to persistent demands for linguistically homogeneous provinces, fostering secessionist trends.

- **1973's Economic Crisis:** Starting in 1973, India experienced a sharp decline in economic conditions, marked by rising unemployment, rampant inflation, and shortages of essential commodities, creating a severe crisis.

The external challenges faced by the nation at the time included:

- **Global Cold War Tensions:** The prevailing global order was characterized by tensions from the Cold War. Many developing nations aligned with either the USA or the Soviet Union. India, however, pursued a Non-Aligned Policy, steering clear of Cold War politics to focus on internal development.

- **Hostile Neighbors:** India faced conflicts with its neighbors, engaging in wars with Pakistan in 1965 and 1971 and with China in 1962. These conflicts not only impeded India's growth but also contributed to regional instability.

In response, India embraced a mixed economy approach, blending socialist principles with elements of capitalism.

Strategic policies, including the implementation of Five-Year Plans, prioritized industrialization, agricultural reforms, and infrastructure development to propel economic growth.

In the late 15th century, European powers, including the Dutch, French, Portuguese, and British, developed a keen interest in the Indian subcontinent. Their motivations were driven by the desire to control valuable resources and trade routes, particularly those associated with spices, textiles, and tea. The British emerged as the dominant power in the region, formally declaring crown rule in 1858 after quelling a significant nationalist uprising known as the Sepoy Mutiny. The ensuing 90 years were marked by tumultuous events that significantly impacted India and the global landscape.

The Indian National Congress (INC), the largest political party in India, was established shortly after 1885 and played a central role in the independence movement. Although the party's ideology was initially ambiguous, World War I became a pivotal moment. India contributed over 1.5 million troops to British war efforts, resulting in more than 45,000 casualties and severe economic strain on India. Despite hopes that Indian participation in the war would lead to increased sovereignty, this did not materialize. The post-World War I period saw a transformation of the INC into a prominent independence movement, representing both Muslim and Hindu voices. Key figures in this movement included Jawaharlal Nehru, Mohandas Gandhi, and Muhammad Ali Jinnah.

Gandhi, who had briefly resided in South Africa after completing law school, returned to India in 1915. His experiences with racism as a new lawyer shaped his perspective, inspiring him to advocate for independence through peaceful means.

Similarly, Nehru, a self-professed nationalist and British-educated lawyer, returned to India after completing his education. Jinnah, a Muslim and a recent graduate with a British legal education, worked at the Bombay High Court and emphasized the importance of Hindu-Muslim unity in the quest for independence.

In the aftermath of World War I, escalating tensions and riots between Hindus and Muslims heightened anxiety within the Muslim minority in India. Ideological and political disparities between the two groups reached alarming levels, driven by their respective quests for political and geographical representation.

As these tensions mounted, the Indian National Congress (INC) staunchly asserted its commitment to secularism and the Gandhian concept of Satyagraha, a strategy of peaceful civil disobedience. While intended to be inclusive, this political approach left some Muslims, particularly leaders of the All-India Muslim League, feeling disenchanted. Jinnah, in particular, regarded Satyagraha as a form of political anarchy. Up until this point, Muslims and Hindus had displayed relative unity under the banner of independence, exemplified by the 1916 Lucknow Pact, which established quotas ensuring the representation of Muslims and other minorities in public offices. However, this unity began to erode when Jinnah resigned from the INC due to his disagreement with Satyagraha as a strategy. Jinnah withdrew from politics for the next decade, only re-entering after the 1937 election, during which the Muslim League secured only 6.7

percent of votes and failed to win a majority in any province, even those with a Muslim majority.

This marked a turning point for Jinnah, challenging his long-held belief that Muslims could be safeguarded in a Hindu-majority nation. His new political strategy advocated for a two-state solution, with separate entities for Muslims and Hindus. This shift coincided with Jinnah's evolving Muslim identity, departing from his earlier stance of broad secularism.

Calls for independence intensified during and after World War II as Indian soldiers participated in the conflict on behalf of the British. The Congress Party expressed its disapproval through a campaign of civil disobedience against the British, leading to the arrests of both Gandhi and Nehru.

During their incarceration, Jinnah solidified support from the Muslim community, positioning himself as the steadfast protector of Muslims in the subcontinent. As World War II concluded, interreligious violence between Hindus and Muslims surged. Public animosity between Gandhi and Jinnah, coupled with provocative speeches by regional politicians, further fueled communal tensions. Muslims and Hindus vied for control of historically religiously diverse neighborhoods, creating an uncertain future where each side held the other responsible for the prevailing uncertainty.

The attempt at a two-state solution did not effectively address internal tensions between India and Pakistan. Despite India's constitutional commitment to secularism, a surge in strict adherence to Hindu and Islamic identities was particularly evident in the 1990s. Communal riots involving Hindus, Muslims,

Sikhs, and Christians persisted across the country from the time of independence. The Kashmir conflict further heightened these tensions. During this period, the ideology of Hindutva, a political movement embracing Hindu fundamentalism and identity, gained prominence. Simultaneously, Islamic extremism saw increased popularity, not only within Kashmir but also extending across India and Pakistan.

The ascent of Hindu nationalism and the increased prominence of the Bharatiya Janata Party (BJP) have far-reaching implications for India's relationship with nuclear-armed Pakistan. The prevailing trend suggests that Hindu nationalists adopt a more assertive stance on security matters, particularly concerning Muslims and Pakistan, which heightens the risk of potential conflict initiation, notably in Kashmir.

One particularly disconcerting aspect is the perspective shared by both Pakistan and India regarding the utilization of first-strike capabilities. Typically, nuclear powers adhere to the norm of employing nuclear weapons solely in response to a first strike, a principle commonly known as mutually assured destruction (MAD). This mutual understanding serves as a deterrent, as both sides anticipate retaliation, discouraging the actual use of nuclear weapons. On the other hand, Pakistan has consistently deviated from this norm by maintaining a stance supporting the consideration of a first-use policy for nuclear weapons. In contrast, India traditionally held that it would only employ nuclear weapons in a second-strike, or retaliatory, scenario. However, there appears to be a shift in this stance since Modi's election in 2014. In their election manifesto of 2014, the BJP expressed a commitment to studying, revising, and reconsidering India's nuclear program. The party also criticized the Indian National Congress (INC) for diminishing the nuclear advancements made during the BJP government in 1999. Under the INC, the focus of the nuclear program had shifted toward civilian energy rather than defense-related expenditures.

While the exact intent of the manifesto remains unclear, many nuclear scholars interpret the language as a discernible hardline shift in Indian foreign policy. The BJP further redefined the concept of "first use," asserting that the assembly, not just the launch, of nuclear weapons by the other side would be considered an initiating response. The willingness of two nuclear powers to entertain the notion of a first strike significantly heightens the risks of miscalculation.

Given the history of recurrent conflicts in the region, even when both countries possessed nuclear weapons, it raises concerns about the effectiveness of nuclear deterrence in the Indian subcontinent. Today, India is home to one of the world's largest Muslim populations, numbering around two hundred million, yet they constitute a minority in this predominantly Hindu country. Despite constitutional protections, Muslims in India have faced systematic discrimination, prejudice, and violence since the country gained independence.

Observers argue that anti-Muslim sentiments have escalated under the leadership of Prime Minister Narendra Modi and the ruling Bharatiya Janata Party (BJP), which has pursued a Hindu nationalist agenda since coming to power in 2014. Following Modi's reelection in 2019, the government has implemented controversial policies criticized for explicitly neglecting the rights of Muslims, aiming to disenfranchise millions of them. During

Modi's tenure, incidents of violence against Muslims have become more frequent, leading to widespread protests within India and drawing condemnation from the international community. India is characterized by a rich tapestry of religious, ethnic, and linguistic diversity. The approximately two hundred million Muslims, primarily identifying as Sunni, constitute the largest minority group, making up roughly 15 percent of the population.

Hindus, comprising about 80 percent of the population, form the majority. Within the Muslim communities in the country, there exists a considerable diversity marked by variations in language, caste, and ethnicity, as well as disparities in access to political and economic influence.

In conclusion, India's journey since gaining independence in 1947 has been marked by a complex interplay of secularism, diversity, and challenges. The distinctive approach to secularism in India, with its nuanced coexistence of religious and state affairs, remains a subject of ongoing debate.

The nation's commitment to protecting minority rights and fostering pluralism, as well as its constitutional safeguards, reflects a unique path in navigating its diverse religious landscape. However, the persistence of issues such as communal violence, discrimination, and religious identity politics underscores the ongoing struggles within this dynamic nation. As India continues to grapple with these complexities, the future will likely see ongoing efforts to strike a balance between upholding its secular values and addressing the diverse needs of its population.

Chapter 5: The Rise of Extremism

Hindu terrorism, sometimes labeled as *Hindutva* **terror** or colloquially referred to as **saffron terror**, denotes acts of terrorism rooted in motivations broadly linked to Hindu nationalism or the ideology of Hindutva.

These acts are primarily attributed to individuals who are affiliated with, or alleged to be associated with, Hindu nationalist organizations such as Rashtriya Swayamsevak Sangh or Abhinav Bharat.

The phenomenon gained significant attention and became a contentious topic in political discourse, particularly in the aftermath of the 2007–2008 attacks that specifically targeted Pakistanis and Muslims within India. The implications of these events sparked discussions on the role of extremist ideologies and their impact on communal relations, prompting a deeper examination of the intersection between religion, nationalism, and acts of violence within the Indian socio-political landscape.

According to Nikita Saxena's article in The Caravan, the term "Hindu terrorism" gained prominence following the 2007 Samjhauta Express bombings and the 2008 Malegaon blasts. The use of this term was notably highlighted by Indian National Congress (Congress) member Digvijaya Singh during a campaign in 2007.

While those responsible for these acts often justify them by citing their Hindu faith, some writers prefer the term "Hindutva terrorism." Subhash Ghatade, a writer and activist, emphasizes that many critics avoid labeling it as "Hindu terrorism" and instead use the term "Hindutva terrorism." On the contrary, political scientist Jyotirmaya Sharma argues against the existence of "Hindu terrorism," asserting that the perpetrators do not represent the Hindu faith.

The Bharatiya Janata Party (BJP) and the Rashtriya Swayamsevak Sangh maintain the stance that Hindu terrorism is a non-existent concept, contending that "Terrorism and Hindus are an oxymoron and can never be related to each other." Journalist and BJP leader Balbir Punj suggests that the term "Hindu terror" was coined and employed by the Congress party post the 2007–2008 incidents as a means to discredit their political adversaries as terrorists. In his 2018 book, "Hindu Terror: Insider Account of Ministry of Home Affairs," former Home Ministry officer Ramaswamy Venkata Subra Mani alleges that the United Progressive Alliance (UPA) government compelled Home Ministry officials to fabricate a narrative about the existence of "Hindu terror."

However, the BJP's narrative has faced scrutiny, particularly in 2019, with revelations that the Multi-Agency Centre established a focus group narrowly focused on investigating terror funding "for Islamist & Sikh Terrorism" only. This occurred despite historical terrorism cases involving individuals associated with Hindu nationalist groups, including Pragya Thakur and Aseemanand, who have been arrested and tried.

Coined in 2002 by the Indian journalist Praveen Swami in the aftermath of the 2002 Gujarat riots, the term "saffron terror" gained significant traction, especially following the 2007–2008 attacks. These attacks, which targeted Pakistanis and Muslims, were reportedly instigated by individuals affiliated with Hindu nationalist organizations like Rashtriya Swayamsevak Sangh and Abhinav Bharat. The term "saffron terror" draws its significance from the symbolic use of the saffron color by several Hindu nationalist groups. Saffron, a vibrant and sacred hue in Hinduism, has been adopted as a symbol of religious and cultural identity. However, the term took on a more contentious connotation as it became associated with acts of violence linked to individuals or groups espousing Hindu nationalist ideologies.

The adoption of this term reflects not only the specific incidents surrounding the 2007–2008 attacks but also the broader discourse on the intersection of religion, politics, and violence in the context of India's diverse cultural landscape. It serves as a descriptor for acts perceived to be carried out by those aligned with Hindu nationalist sentiments and ideologies, adding a layer of complexity to discussions on religious identity, extremism, and the evolving socio-political dynamics within the country.

The 2002 Gujarat riots, often termed the 2002 Gujarat violence, unfolded over a tumultuous three-day period marked by severe inter-communal clashes in the western Indian state of Gujarat. The tragic catalyst for these events was the burning of a train in Godhra on February 27, 2002, leading to the heartbreaking loss of 58 Hindu pilgrims and karsevaks who were returning from Ayodhya. This incident is widely recognized as the flashpoint that set off the subsequent chain of violence.

After the initial eruption of riots, Ahmedabad experienced persistent outbreaks of violence for three months. Throughout the state, there were sustained instances of violence targeting the minority Muslim population for the following year. In 2012, the then Chief Minister, Narendra Modi, was cleared of complicity in the violence by a Special Investigation Team (SIT) appointed by the Supreme Court of India. The SIT also dismissed allegations that the state government had inadequately acted to prevent the riots. However, these findings were met with incredulity and discontent within the Muslim community.

In July 2013, disturbing allegations emerged, suggesting that the SIT had suppressed vital evidence related to the events. In December of the same year, an Indian court upheld the original SIT report and rejected a petition seeking Modi's prosecution. By April 2014, the Supreme Court expressed satisfaction with the SIT's investigations in nine cases related to the violence and dismissed a plea contesting the SIT report as "baseless."

Despite the official classification as a communalist riot, numerous scholars have characterized the events of 2002 as a pogrom. Some analysts argue that the attacks were premeditated, with the train burning to serve as a "staged trigger" for planned violence. Others assert that these events meet the "legal definition of genocide" and describe them as instances of state terrorism or ethnic cleansing. Significant incidents of mass violence include the Naroda Patiya massacre near a police training camp, the Gulbarg Society massacre, where former parliamentarian Ehsan Jafri was among the victims, and various incidents in Vadodara city.

Scholars delving into the 2002 riots contend that they were premeditated acts constituting a form of ethnic cleansing.

They point to allegations of complicity by the state government and law enforcement in the violence that unfolded, thereby underscoring the complex and controversial nature of the events and their aftermath within the socio-political fabric of Gujarat. The ascent of Hindu nationalism has transformative implications for international relations, altering the trajectory set by Nehru's foreign policy during the Cold War, characterized by nonalignment and substantial investment in global institutions like the UN. Despite the end of the Cold War, India retained its distance from the United States, forging military alliances with other nations.

In contrast, the US cultivated closer ties with Pakistan and China. In 2009, under Obama's pivot to Asia strategy, India and the US initiated a shift toward warmer relations, with the US advocating for India's permanent seat on the UN Security Council. This pivot, motivated by the US's interest in countering China's growing regional and global influence, marked a significant diplomatic realignment.

An intriguing turn in the US–India relationship occurred in 2016 during the US election when Hindu nationalist parties rallied behind Republican candidate Donald Trump. These groups were energized by Trump's perceived tough stance on Muslim immigration and terrorism. Hindu nationalist parties, such as Shiv Sena and the VHP, organized large public prayer ceremonies for Trump.

Trump, recognizing his popularity among certain segments of the Indian population, incorporated this support into his campaign. Notably, Shalabh Kumar, Chairman of the Trump campaign's Indian American Advisory Council, used a Trump campaign ad appealing to American Hindus, featuring Hindu symbology and music, and concluding with Trump speaking in

Hindi with the slogan "Ab ki baar, Trump sarkar," mirroring Modi's 2014 campaign slogan. Trump's alignment with Hindu nationalists may also be interpreted as an effort to counter Islamic extremism in Pakistan. From India's perspective, Trump's rhetoric and ties to Hindu nationalists indicate tacit support for a firm stance against Pakistan. In late 2017, Trump's decision to withhold military aid to Pakistan, citing its role as a haven for terrorists, was applauded by India and represented a substantial departure from decades of US military and economic support for Pakistan.

The potential influence of Hindu nationalism extends beyond India's borders, as some nationalists envision an expanded Indian map to encompass Nepal, Bhutan, Afghanistan, Pakistan, and Bangladesh. This sentiment has manifested in a campaign to revise Indian textbooks and maps to reflect what these groups deem as the rightful borders. While India's constitution upholds secularism, the prevailing trend over the past three decades suggests a shift toward Hindu nationalism.

Nehru's vision of a peaceful, multireligious state faces challenges, and the success of the Hindu Nationalist Party raises questions about India's future trajectory, particularly regarding its relations with neighboring countries and its commitment to secular principles. The unfolding scenario may answer the lingering doubts that Jinnah maintained regarding the nature of the Indian state.

Chapter 6: Contemporary Challenges for Indian Muslims

Since the BJP government assumed power in 2014, it has implemented stringent measures that have been criticized for marginalizing minority communities in India, particularly Muslims. Examples include the **Citizenship Amendment Bill**, which expedites citizenship for non-Muslim migrants from neighboring countries, and the controversial revocation of Articles 370 and 35A in Kashmir (Disputed Territory).

There are concerns about the alleged oppression of Muslims there, drawing parallels to the situation in Palestine. Both India and Israel have been accused of engaging in land grabbing and perpetuating a humanitarian crisis in regions with Muslim populations.

The longstanding issues of Palestine and Kashmir remain critical items on the United Nations Security Council (UNSC) agenda. Numerous instances of international law violations and disregard for the Geneva Conventions in disputed Kashmir and Palestine have been condemned.

The conflict between Israel and Palestine has also sparked apprehensions about the escalation of Islamophobia globally, including in India. This necessitates a collective response from the international community, Muslim-majority states, and the Organization of Islamic Cooperation (OIC) to condemn discriminatory actions. The recent diplomatic ties between some Arab states and India underscore the importance of these nations leveraging their influence to encourage New Delhi to mitigate anti-Muslim sentiments and refrain from policies that fuel Islamophobia. Addressing these concerns is crucial for fostering social cohesion within societies.

After a decade of BJP governance in India, there is a growing influence of communal forces, particularly impacting the lives of minorities, especially Muslims. Regrettably, the trend of anti-Muslim violence is expected to persist as the Sangh Parivar deploys its supporters to ensure electoral success for the BJP.

The question arises whether the BJP, provided it forms the next government, will continue with politics of polarization and animosity and perpetuate the portrayal of Indian Muslims as perpetual outsiders, subjecting them to conversion or relegating them to second-class citizenship in the nation. Unfortunately, available evidence suggests the likelihood of such a scenario. Despite this, India's ostensibly secular parties have not been sufficiently vocal in condemning anti-Muslim hate.

Systematically, the *Sangh Parivar* seems intent on dismantling the rich history of Muslim civilization in India, spanning a millennium. This ambitious project aims to erase all traces of Muslim culture from India's societal fabric.

While this endeavor presents significant challenges, the *Sangh's* supporters are dedicated to this cause. The vilification of Indian Muslims is just one facet of this extensive campaign. The sinister plan also includes the demolition of mosques, replaced by temples, while the *Sangh* endorses violence against Indian Muslims as a purported means to 'punish' them for the real or perceived transgressions of medieval Muslim rulers. The increasing intolerance toward Muslims in India is underscored by findings from various external sources. Washington DC-based think tank Freedom House has labeled India as 'partially free,' shedding light on the erosion of democracy in the country. While numerous forms of state repression and authoritarianism are at play, the focus here is on the plight of Indian Muslims.

The Council on Foreign Relations, another influential think tank, rightly points out that Muslims not only face the brunt of communal violence in India but also endure discrimination in areas such as employment, housing, and education.

Scholars Christophe Jaffrelot and Maulik Saini, writing for The Indian Express, highlight the underrepresentation of Muslims, constituting over 14% of the population, in the public sector.

Government statistics reveal a significant increase in Muslim unemployment from 2.62% in 2009-10 to 7.16% in 2018-19.[2]

Apart from institutional and economic bias, active persecution of Muslims is evident, with an Indian NGO, Common Cause, finding pervasive anti-Muslim bias among surveyed police respondents. Hindu nationalists targeting Muslims often enjoy widespread impunity.

Extreme examples of communal hatred include the creation of 'anti-Romeo squads' to prevent 'love jihad' and public lynching of Muslims suspected of cow-related offenses, actions that find support from prominent BJP leaders. Criticism abounds for Prime Minister Modi's Citizenship Amendment Act of 2019, excluding Muslim migrants from expedited citizenship. The controversial

---

[2]https://indianexpress.com/article/opinion/columns/a-workforce-less-diverse-muslims-in-public-and-private-sector-8094176/

revocation of Kashmir's special status and the decision to allow non-permanent residents to vote in Kashmiri elections add to the unrest. Unjustifiably, the Modi government increased assembly seats in the Hindu-majority Jammu area while neglecting the Muslim-majority Kashmir valley.

Despite India's geopolitical significance and growing global prominence, concerns over its democratic credentials have intensified during Modi's tenure.

Genocide Watch warns of the potential genocide of Indian Muslims, urging global attention.

The US Congress Commission on International Religious Freedom has sought for three years to place India on a list of 'countries of particular concern.'

While Pakistan expresses concern about the mistreatment of Indian Muslims, its limited affluence and international leverage hinder its ability to draw attention to India's intolerance.

Additionally, Pakistan's poor record of discrimination against religious minorities diminishes the impact of its warnings. Despite the controversy surrounding the US acting as a moral arbiter, it remains a key player capable of influencing India to reconsider its current trajectory.

Northern India, with a significant Muslim population residing in Uttar Pradesh and surrounding regions, grapples with persistent challenges hindering the community's access to quality education and socio-economic advancement. Following are the challenges faced by Muslims in Northern India:

Socio-Economic Disparities:

The Muslim community experiences pronounced socio-economic disparities, particularly in rural areas, resulting in limited access to quality education. Implementing targeted socio-economic development programs remains crucial. Initiatives such as skill development, entrepreneurship support, and enhanced employment opportunities can uplift the community and create a conducive environment for quality education.

Lack of Quality Educational Institutions Managed by Muslims:

Northern India grapples with an insufficient number of quality educational institutions managed by Muslims, hindering the educational progression of the community. Mobilizing successful Muslim entrepreneurs to establish and support quality schools is paramount.

Collaboration with the government, formulation of supportive policies, and partnerships with NGOs and private organizations can expedite the establishment of these much-needed educational institutions.

Lack of Female Education:

Cultural and social barriers impede Muslim girls' access to quality education, perpetuating gender disparities. A multi-faceted approach involving community outreach targeted awareness campaigns, provision of scholarships, the establishment of girls' hostels, safe transportation, and potentially introducing segregated sections for girls within schools can collectively empower and encourage Muslim girls to pursue education.

Language Barriers:

Language differences between home and the school's medium of instruction pose a significant hurdle for many Muslims in northern India. Promoting bilingual education in schools can facilitate a smoother transition, bridging the linguistic gap and ensuring better comprehension and learning outcomes for students.

Lack of Scholarships and Financial Support:

Limited financial resources hinder the pursuit of higher education among Muslim youth. The introduction of scholarships and financial aid programs specifically tailored for Muslim students is imperative. Encouraging philanthropic efforts from within the Muslim community can play a pivotal role in ensuring that higher education becomes more accessible.

Community Awareness and Participation:

Engaging in community-driven awareness programs, encouraging parental involvement, and establishing community-based education committees can collectively contribute to enhancing the quality of education at the grassroots level.

Social Stigma:

Prejudice and social stigma against the Muslim community create psychological barriers to pursuing quality education. Promoting interfaith dialogues, cultural exchanges, and initiatives fostering social inclusion and harmony can counteract social stigma. Schools should actively encourage an environment of tolerance and diversity to create a supportive atmosphere for all students. Comprehensive, community-focused strategies are essential to address the multifaceted education challenges faced by the Muslim community in northern India.

Bridging socio-economic disparities, empowering the community to establish educational institutions, promoting inclusivity, removing gender barriers, addressing language issues, providing financial support, and fostering community awareness are integral components of a holistic approach.

By collectively embracing these measures, northern India can pave the way for the socio-economic upliftment and overall development of its

Muslim population through enhanced educational opportunities. In conclusion, the challenges faced by the Muslim community in northern India, particularly in Uttar Pradesh, demand urgent attention and comprehensive solutions.

From the implementation of stringent measures to marginalize minorities to the socio-economic disparities hindering access to quality education, the issues are complex and intertwined.

It is imperative for stakeholders, including the international community, to collaborate and address these challenges collectively.

Through targeted socio-economic development, the establishment of quality educational institutions, the promotion of female education, the addressing of language barriers, the provision of financial support, and the fostering of community awareness, there is hope for positive change.

The inclusivity of all communities and the protection of minority rights are essential for building a harmonious and prosperous society in northern India. Only through concerted efforts can the region overcome its current obstacles and pave the way for a more equitable and inclusive future.

Chapter 7: Resistance and Resilience

The pursuit of identity is driving many young individuals toward divisive ideologies, particularly evident in the Middle East (West Asia) and Afghanistan, which have become focal points for foreign fighters motivated by jihadi fervor.

Despite challenges in conflict zones like Gaza, preventing direct involvement, the determination and influence of these individuals persist. This pattern reflects past scenarios in Chechnya, Syria-Iraq, and Afghanistan, where numerous ideologically indoctrinated foreign fighters engaged in complex conflicts framed through a religious lens.

Jihadi groups adeptly exploit narratives of suffering, distorting religion to recruit members. Individuals from places as distant as France and the Maldives are enticed by the prospect of contributing to a greater cause, volunteering for conflicts about which they may have limited knowledge. At its peak, approximately two-thirds of ISIS fighters were foreign combatants.

In certain parts of the Muslim world, where faith deeply permeates everyday life, a susceptible segment finds itself easily drawn to provocative jihadi rhetoric. This vulnerability can be attributed to factors ranging from globalization to pan-Islamism rooted in the shared cause of 'Ummah'—the global Muslim collective.

Pan-Islamism, a political concept, underscores the unity of the 'Ummah' and aims to cultivate a robust, deterritorialized communal identity, often leading to self-identification with struggles framed through a religious lens. Simultaneously, hybrid influences on Islam contribute to a resurgence of rigid, doctrinaire interpretations within more puritanical segments of the population. This creates fertile ground for jihadi ideologies, perceived as unique in their crusade to uphold 'religious purity.' The Islamic foundation of the state conveniently serves as a pretext for such radical self-justifications, providing a semblance of legitimacy to these perilous rationalizations.

In the Western context, challenges with immigrant assimilation can be traced to the struggle faced by immigrant communities in this regard. The assimilation process, if left to free agency, often spans three to four generations and several decades. Each generation navigates this journey uniquely. First-generation immigrants typically embark on their journey seeking economic opportunities, but their sense of identity remains deeply rooted in their homelands. With close familial ties and cultural bonds, their migration is often seen as a hopeful voyage.

However, the second generation finds themselves in an identity limbo. They have limited familial or cultural connections with their ancestral lands, and they feel alienated in their adopted homelands due to prejudices and cultural differences. Caught between two worlds, they struggle to define their identity. It is in their quest to belong that Jihadi propaganda, with its clear calls to action, finds a receptive audience. Promising a noble cause and a place in a larger-than-life schema provides them with power and purpose, filling the voids in their identity.

Noteworthy examples include the radical English-speaking cleric Anwar al-Awlaki, Al-Qaida's recruiter and propagandist-in-chief in the West, as well as individuals like Hasib Hussain, the youngest among the 7/7 London bombers, and the Kouachi brothers, Chérif and Saïd, responsible for the Charlie Hebdo attack in Paris in 2015—all of whom were second-generation immigrants struggling with assimilation. Despite the evident correlation between non-assimilation and radicalization, Western societies have been reluctant to address the issue. This reluctance stems from a misjudged conviction that immigrants should be allowed the liberty to assimilate at their own pace for comfort with the integration process.

In India, the emphasis on national identity supersedes religious affiliations, with 'being Indian' taking precedence over sectarian distinctions. The Indian Muslim identity is deeply rooted in history and heritage rather than overt religiosity or strict adherence to codes of faith. The Indian experience showcases a harmonious interplay between Sufi saints and the Bhakti movement, giving rise to a syncretic spiritual ecosystem.

In the southern regions, Hindu Zamorin rulers fostered an environment where Muslims and Hindus not only freely intermarried but also upheld their distinct traditions. A prime example is the revered Muslim saint Vavar, who receives ritualistic respect from the devotees of the Hindu god Ayyappa, with millions visiting his shrine each year. Figures like Sai Baba of Shirdi, Moinuddin Chishti of Ajmer, Sant Namdev of Narsi, and Neem Karoli Baba of Kainchi have amassed millions of followers across the religious spectrum.

These multi-faith spaces serve as melting pots of cultures, values, and beliefs, nurturing a syncretic social fabric that reinforces collective identities founded on accommodativeness and inclusion. This amalgamation mitigates the inclination toward insular identities. Significantly, in India, this dynamic has led to a collective community effort in vigilance against radicalization, enhancing resilience against jihadi indoctrination. Complementing these efforts are both visible and quantifiable elements. On one front, assertive policy interventions concentrate on capacity building and economic upliftment. Initiatives like Pradhan Mantri Virasat Ka Samvardhan (PMVIKAS) and supportive financial mechanisms from agencies such as the National Minorities Development and Finance Corporation (NMDFC) exemplify this focus. These endeavors specifically target the most marginalized and undereducated segments of the community, who are likely more susceptible to jihadi rhetoric.

On the other front, narratives of prosperity and achievement are emphasized, highlighting the visibility of Muslim success across various sectors of Indian society, including government, business, entertainment, finance, and politics. These narratives challenge the notion of disenfranchisement, offering little on-ground validation for jihadi rationalizations. Despite Muslims constituting approximately 14 percent of India's population and representing over 10 percent of Muslims globally, the community has shown resilience against jihadi propaganda. This resilience underscores the influence of India's cohesive national identity in countering divisive rhetoric.

Ruskin Bond succinctly captures the essence of the Indian identity in his 2002 essay, "On Being an Indian," stating, "Race did not make me one. Religion did not make me one. But history did. And in the long run, it's history that counts."

National identity encompasses self-categorization and the associated experiences. Substantive national identities, exemplified by countries like India, foster positive self-categorization and have demonstrated their efficacy in diminishing the allure of destructive ideologies. The varying levels of susceptibility to radicalization across different societies underscore the importance of robust national identities that overshadow narrow, self-serving ideologies.

The West could draw valuable lessons from experiences like India's, which contribute to building societal resilience, and from Singapore's, which accelerates this process. Singapore, through carefully crafted school curricula highlighting the diverse culture of its population and initiatives like the Ethnic Integration Program aimed at breaking communal enclaves, has successfully nurtured cross-cultural understanding, fostering a strengthened national identity within a compressed timeframe. These endeavors have diminished the appeal of jihadi propaganda, with relatively few Singaporeans joining the ranks of foreign fighters, despite the growth of its immigrant population.

As old battlegrounds dissipate, returning radicalized fighters are met with varying receptions upon their arrival home. However, akin to the viper in Aesop's fable "The Farmer and the Viper," which bit the farmer after being saved from the winter chill, it is only a matter of time before some of these returning fighters pose a threat to the communities attempting to rehabilitate them, thus creating new battlegrounds domestically. Estimates indicate that anywhere from 11 percent to 26 percent of returning fighters revert to engaging in terrorism. At the heart of this challenge lies the quest for identity, underscoring the urgent need for nations to construct stronger, more inclusive identities capable of resisting the allure of divisive ideologies. As we contemplate the future in the ongoing battle against religious extremism, a pivotal question emerges: *How can nations construct resilient, inclusive identities that withstand the seductive calls of radical ideologies?* How we address this question will shape our collective ability to forge a future that transcends the narrow confines of sectarianism and hatred.

Some of the respectable people who can help us in this regard are the faith leaders. Faith leaders, encompassing individuals of all genders, are those acknowledged by their faith community, whether through formal recognition or informal acknowledgment, as holding authoritative and influential leadership positions within faith institutions. Their role is to guide, inspire, or lead others within the context of their faith community.

It is commonly asserted that Islam lacks religious authority; however, the reality is that numerous figures assume this role. This diversity is evident in the various terms used to designate religious experts, such as *Ulamas*, *Imams*, and others.

The primary objective of this narrative is to offer the reader an understanding of the nature, complexity, and significance of Islamic leadership, exploring the concepts and principles that underpin it. These qualities distinguish Islamic leadership from other leadership paradigms.

The fundamental sources guiding Islamic leadership for Muslim leaders are the Al-Qur'an and Hadith. Sub-topics related to Islamic leadership delve into all the attributes—traits, skills, power, and authority—required by leaders. Faith holds a distinct place in our lives, especially concerning how we treat others with the same respect we desire. During times of profound anxiety, faith can serve as a significant source of comfort and community resilience. Religious leaders play a vital role in most communities, traditionally serving as influential figures within the clerisy, religious institutions, mosques, churches, or governments, playing prominent roles within their communities or nations.

Religious leaders and faith communities stand as the largest and most well-organized civil institutions globally, commanding the allegiance of billions of believers and bridging divisions of race, class, and nationality. Among civil society representatives, religious leaders possess extensive experience in establishing and collaborating on international partnerships, making their expertise invaluable to the global breastfeeding effort.

Often revered as the most respected figures in their communities, religious leaders wield considerable influence in shaping attitudes, opinions, and behaviors within their respective faiths. Members trust them, and both community members and political leaders |end attentive ears to their counsel. Particularly at the family and community levels, religious leaders possess the authority to raise awareness and impact attitudes, behaviors, and practices, aligning them with faith-based teachings.

At these crucial levels, religious leaders can:

•	Motivate and educate followers to adopt additional healthy behaviors in harmony with religious teachings.

•	Intentionally leverage the commonality of religious Holy Texts within communities to effect change within political and religious systems, actively promoting the work of The Common Word and the Charter of Compassion.

- Affirm and vocalize support for the universal right to religious freedom of expression and practice worldwide.

- Religious leaders, armed with courage and vision, assume a unique role in uniting people around the shared values of our common humanity. Their influence extends to guiding cultural and social norms and fostering practices that reflect these universal values.

Therefore, the complex dynamics of identity, assimilation challenges, and the global battle against extremism underscore the need for inclusive and resilient national identities. Learning from diverse experiences, such as India's harmonious cultural amalgamation, nations can strengthen their identities against divisive ideologies.

As the world grapples with returning radicalized fighters and the persistent quest for identity, the role of faith leaders emerges as pivotal. Their influence and ability to shape attitudes make them valuable allies in promoting inclusive identities that transcend sectarianism and hatred.

Nations must leverage the wisdom and guidance of faith leaders to construct resilient, inclusive identities, fostering a future characterized by unity and understanding.

Chapter 8: The Global Context

Despite facing numerous domestic challenges like healthcare, education, and the economy, the Indian government remains dedicated to addressing these issues and implementing policies aimed at enhancing the well-being and prosperity of its people. India's G20 priorities underscore its commitment to inclusive and resilient growth, with a focus on climate, finance, sustainable development, and global health resilience.

India advocates for a gradual and systematic approach to sustainable development and reducing carbon emissions, ensuring support for the most vulnerable segments of society.

Recognizing the significant threat posed by climate change to its environment, economy, and populace, India's efforts in this regard are measured and balanced, taking into consideration the diverse needs and circumstances of its population. It's essential to acknowledge that democratically elected governments have both the right and responsibility to pursue the welfare of their citizens.

India, maintaining its status as the world's largest democracy, boasts a vibrant and diverse civil society, notwithstanding challenges to freedom of expression and accountability, typical of any nation. Various organizations and individuals are actively engaged in fostering transparency and fairness in both governance and society.

Rooted in a rich history and culture, India showcases resilience, innovation, and leadership, shaping its current and prospective role on the global stage. While hurdles persist,

India's potential and contributions to the international community should not be discounted based solely on certain political perceptions or allegations. Sustained advancement and investment in its people and society will empower India to continue playing a pivotal role in driving global advancement and prosperity for years ahead.

As the world grapples with the aftermath of the COVID-19 pandemic that marred the year 2020, the arduous path to recovery looms large over many nations in the coming year. India, in particular, faces significant challenges as it navigates through the ongoing crisis, especially in managing the impact on its most vulnerable populations. Additionally, the country is confronted with another formidable challenge - the persistent military tensions with China, which pose a substantial threat given their scale and geographic significance.

These dual challenges could arguably be considered some of the most pressing security concerns India has encountered since the 1971 war with Pakistan, culminating in the birth of independent Bangladesh. Moreover, numerous other pressing issues demand the government's attention, including internal security threats such as terrorism, the longstanding Maoist insurgency, and the persistent communal and sectarian unrest that poses a threat to the social fabric of the nation.

Despite efforts to bolster its military capabilities, the bleak economic forecast, particularly regarding the overall GDP, is expected to constrain defense expenditure in real terms, thereby adversely affecting India's military modernization endeavors. This precarious economic outlook is likely to impact India's capacity to maintain a robust stance against China. Calls for the

United States to strengthen its strategic ties with India stem from the perception of New Delhi as a counterbalance to China in Asia and a natural democratic partner in the region. However, even if such an alliance were to materialize, it would not mirror the Cold War-era alliances with Europe and Japan. The Trump administration's tenure significantly weakened U.S. soft power and regional hegemony while China expanded its economic and military influence. European allies no longer view Washington as an entirely reliable partner, and doubts persist regarding the viability of 'the Quad' as a robust multinational alternative to China.

For instance, post-COVID-19, the Japanese economy suffered. Also, with Shinzo Abe leaving office, enthusiasm for the Quad alliance had waned. India, at the time, was focusing more on bilateral partnerships to deal with China.

In this way, India's role in the UN Security Council eventually offered a chance to improve relations with China, which further influenced its actions on issues like counterterrorism. Such multilateral approaches helped ease regional tensions.

Although India's traditional stance prioritizes internal affairs, recent administrations have recognized the necessity of engaging with the global community to meet domestic goals. While the rhetoric may emphasize an inward focus, India's actions increasingly demonstrate an outward orientation. Over the years, India has significantly broadened its military, diplomatic, and economic endeavors beyond the confines of Nehru's Non-Aligned stance.

India's foreign policy revolves around five main priorities: ensuring security, driving economic growth, securing energy resources, managing nuclear capabilities, and enhancing global prestige.

In terms of security, India focuses on protecting its borders and combating internal threats. Economically, it aims to grow by attracting investments and expanding trade, especially with countries like the United States. Energy security is vital, as India relies heavily on imports and seeks to diversify its sources while considering environmental impacts.

India maintains nuclear capabilities for deterrence but supports nonproliferation efforts. Lastly, India aims for global recognition, leveraging its diverse democracy and strategic partnerships, notably with the U.S.

In its relationships with China and the U.S., India balances cooperation with competition. While tensions exist with China over territorial disputes, India seeks closer ties with the U.S., sharing common interests in areas like counterterrorism and regional stability.

Given India's five principal strategic interests, as it finds its position in the world and lives up to the potential that its character and natural assets imply, it could become a powerful force for transformation. In the short to medium term, India's potential for becoming an agent of change is significant in several key areas.

Considering its impressive military and soft-power capabilities, as India builds confidence and finds its voice, I anticipate that it will become more active in helping to create a regional security regime and in pushing stability outward. As Indian expatriate communities gain prominence due to their growing size and economic influence, host countries are increasingly recognizing their significance. They are becoming more visible in electoral politics, albeit in small numbers. US President Donald Trump, for instance, has appointed several individuals of Indian origin to key positions in his administration, including Nikki Haley as US Ambassador to the UN and Raj Shah as Deputy Assistant and Research Director.

In Europe, leaders like Leo Varadkar in Ireland and Antonio Costa in Portugal, both second-generation migrants from India, serve as prime ministers in their respective countries. Modi has effectively connected with the diaspora, portraying himself as a catalyst for change in India, a country they left due to corruption and bureaucracy.

Modi sees great potential in their contributions to India's growth, as evident from his vision of transitioning from "brain drain to brain gain," emphasizing a shared dream of *Bharatiyata* (transl. Indianness).

The government's approach to the diaspora is twofold: providing services and protection to Non-Resident Indians (NRIs) and Overseas Citizens of India (OCIs) while also encouraging their contribution to India's development through philanthropy, knowledge sharing, investments, and support for various projects.

Under Modi's leadership, several initiatives have been launched or revamped, such as the 'Know India Program' (KIP) and the establishment of Head Post Offices as passport centers.

Training centers and orientation programs help prepare individuals for overseas employment and minimize cultural differences. Policies have been introduced to safeguard the welfare of Indians abroad, like setting minimum wages for certain job categories and implementing measures to prevent fraudulent contracts.

However, some policies have faced criticism from countries like the UAE for alleged sovereignty breaches.

KIP, initiated by Atal Bihari Vajpayee, has expanded to accommodate more participants each year, particularly focusing on *Girmitiya* youth to deepen their ties with India. Other youth-oriented programs include scholarships for undergraduate studies in Indian universities and online quizzes to enhance knowledge of India's culture and heritage.

Despite criticisms that events like the *Pravasi Bharatiya Divas* primarily attract affluent diaspora members, Modi continues to use them as opportunities to engage with Indian expats.

The dedication of the *Pravasi Bhartiya Kendra* in New Delhi underscores the government's commitment to recognizing diaspora contributions and addressing their concerns, although challenges remain in ensuring inclusive engagement.

In conclusion, India's trajectory on the global stage is marked by resilience, innovation, and leadership, rooted in its rich history and culture.

Despite facing daunting challenges, both domestically and internationally, India continues to demonstrate its potential for driving positive change and contributing meaningfully to global advancement. From navigating complex geopolitical dynamics to harnessing the talents and resources of its diaspora communities, India remains poised to play a pivotal role in shaping the future landscape of international relations. As it continues to address internal disparities and foster inclusive growth, India's influence is set to expand, offering hope for a brighter and more prosperous future for its people and the world at large.

Chapter 9: Toward a Harmonious Future

In light of the well-known diversity in India, it is imperative to underscore the importance of Diversity, Equity, Inclusion, and Belonging (DEIB) in the region. A DEIB-focused environment cultivates a culture where all citizens, irrespective of their ethnic and religious backgrounds, feel respected, included, and empowered to contribute fully. Such an environment not only promotes equity and equality but also drives productivity and innovation.

In today's dynamic landscape, fostering DEIB is essential for nurturing a cohesive and flourishing organization. Embracing diverse gender identities and generations demonstrates a commitment to inclusivity, fostering an environment where every employee feels valued and respected. Addressing unconscious biases directly helps dismantle barriers to collaboration and growth, while proactive steps toward systemic change ensure sustainable progress toward a fair and equitable infrastructure in the country.

Enhanced transparency in setting and communicating DEIB goals fosters accountability and facilitates meaningful progress monitoring. Moreover, supporting citizens' mental health recognizes the importance of holistic well-being, contributing to a compassionate and understanding society.

The advantages of a DEIB-focused environment are manifold. Diverse societies are better equipped to generate innovative solutions and understand the diverse needs of their citizens. Additionally, an inclusive workplace significantly enhances employee morale and productivity. The government can take various steps to foster a more diverse and inclusive workplace. Ensuring fair and equitable practices is critical, as is providing diversity and inclusion training for the natives. Furthermore, governments should create an environment where people feel comfortable expressing their opinions, experiences, and concerns.

Implementing initiatives such as adopting a zero-tolerance policy for discrimination and harassment and providing unconscious bias training can communicate a commitment to valuing every single citizen. The bottom line is that it is our vision to become a globally diverse and inclusive country, embracing the concept of every individual being respected, valued, and empowered to be their authentic selves.

Inclusion is not merely a checkbox but a core belief ingrained in different sectors within the country. By embracing and leveraging our differences, we better understand our citizens' needs, thereby forging stronger connections with our community.

Looking ahead, diversity and inclusion will only grow in importance. As the world becomes increasingly diverse, challenges may abound, but so do opportunities. Together, we can create a more diverse and inclusive society where everyone has the chance to thrive.

One of the vital ways of attaining diversity in the country is through empowerment. Especially the empowerment of the minorities, in the case of India, the empowerment of the Muslim minority. Community empowerment involves several key principles in its execution, including raising awareness within the community, providing education and training, organizing collective efforts, building on existing strengths, and ensuring decision-making power rests with the community itself. It encompasses various aspects of societal life, such as education, economy, socio-cultural dynamics, psychology, and politics, particularly in the context of the digital economy era.

When it comes to the Muslims in India, comparisons can be drawn between current diverse Indian policies and the historical Islamic governance of Umar Ibn Khattab, especially in the educational and economic sectors.

For instance, during Khattab's era as the second caliph, governance was firm yet sensitive to the needs of the people. Policies enacted during this time aimed at benefiting all citizens under his caliphate, irrespective of their religious affiliation.

During his rule, Caliph Umar instituted various reforms across different aspects of governance, including administration, military, social welfare, and religious practices.

In terms of administration, Umar established a special department to address complaints against state officials, ensuring accountability and justice. This department, led by Muhammad ibn Muslimah, acted as an administrative court and conducted thorough investigations into reported misconduct. Those found guilty faced consequences ranging from public humiliation to removal from office. In the military sphere, Umar organized the army as a state department, ensuring efficiency and readiness for defense. He introduced a system of military service for all eligible adults, categorizing them into standing army units and reserves. Pay and allowances were provided regularly, and promotions were based on merit and length of service. Umar also strategically positioned military cantonments throughout the empire to respond swiftly to any threats. Socially, Umar introduced welfare and pension systems through Islamic law, using funds collected through taxes like Zakat to support the needy, including the poor, elderly, widows, and disabled. Additionally, he ordered the stockpiling of food supplies in every region to prepare for disasters or famines, establishing the foundation for what can be considered the world's first major welfare state.

In matters of religion, Umar reinstated the practice of praying tarawih in congregation during the month of Ramadan, which had been discontinued by Prophet Muhammad(PBUH) due to concerns about potential misunderstandings. With the fear alleviated, Umar saw the benefits of communal prayer and encouraged its observance.

Overall, Umar's governance was marked by a commitment to justice, efficiency, social welfare, and religious observance, laying the groundwork for the expansion and stability of the Islamic empire.

These historical policies of community empowerment under his rule serve as a valuable framework for interpretation within the contemporary context. As we navigate the digital age, it becomes imperative to adapt and modify previous policies to ensure their relevance and feasibility in today's realities. Besides timely adaptation, active civic engagement is the cornerstone of a healthy democracy, empowering citizens to voice their concerns and shape the direction of their society. By participating in civic activities, individuals not only contribute to the democratic process but also cultivate a sense of ownership and responsibility in governance.

Furthermore, civic participation strengthens the social fabric by fostering inclusivity, diversity, and cohesion. When people from diverse backgrounds collaborate to tackle common issues, they build a more resilient and dynamic community. Through active involvement in decision-making, citizens ensure that their interests are represented and that policies align with the collective needs of society.

Moreover, civic engagement serves as a vital mechanism for holding elected officials and institutions accountable. By actively participating in democratic processes, citizens exert influence on policy decisions and hold authorities responsible for their actions. This fosters transparency and accountability, ensuring that governance remains responsive to the needs and aspirations of the populace.

Civic participation encompasses more than just voting; it extends to various forms of engagement that shape communities and societies. While voting is a cornerstone of democracy, community service is equally vital. Volunteering at local initiatives such as food banks or clean-up drives fosters solidarity and empathy among citizens, transcending social divides and promoting a shared responsibility for community welfare. Engaging in community service not only benefits those in need but also contributes to the overall betterment of society. It creates a positive impact that reverberates through the lives of others, promoting a culture of compassion and civic responsibility. Advocacy is another essential aspect of civic participation, empowering individuals to advocate for policy changes, raise awareness about pressing issues, and mobilize communities for a cause. Through advocacy efforts, individuals can amplify their voices and influence decision-makers, ensuring that important issues receive the attention they deserve. Moreover, technological advancements have revolutionized civic participation. Social media platforms serve as powerful tools for organizing campaigns, raising awareness, and mobilizing communities. Online petitions, viral campaigns, and digital activism have emerged as effective means of driving social change and holding institutions accountable in the digital age.

Therefore, the vitality of diversity, equity, inclusion, and belonging (DEIB) in India cannot be overstated, as it forms the bedrock of a thriving and inclusive society. Through a commitment to DEIB, India can harness the collective strength of its diverse populace and foster a culture of empathy, solidarity, and civic responsibility.

By drawing inspiration from historical governance under leaders like Umar Ibn Khattab and adapting policies to the modern digital era, India can ensure that every citizen is respected, valued, and empowered to contribute to the nation's progress. Moreover, by embracing active civic engagement in various forms, from voting to community service and advocacy, India can uphold the principles of democracy, hold institutions accountable, and shape a future that celebrates diversity and inclusivity at every level. As we move forward, let us continue to prioritize DEIB and civic participation, recognizing that together, we can build a more diverse, equitable, and inclusive society where every individual has the opportunity to thrive.

Conclusion

As we reflect on the intricacies of human nature and the evolution of societal norms, it becomes apparent that our journey has been marked by both triumphs and challenges. Throughout history, the virtues of equality, justice, and morality have been intrinsic to our collective conscience, guiding us toward a better world.

However, amidst the progress and achievements, we cannot overlook the persistent distractions of injustice, corruption, and exploitation that plague our societies. Despite being bestowed with the gift of conscience, we have often faltered in upholding these fundamental principles.

This book has sought to shed light on these truths, confronting uncomfortable realities and urging us to reevaluate our path forward. It has delved into the transformation of religion from a unifying force to a source of division while also reaffirming the timeless values that bind us together as humans.

As we navigate the complexities of our modern world, may we be inspired to embrace compassion, empathy, and a commitment to the well-being of all. Let us transcend the divisive interpretations of religion and rediscover the common humanity that unites us.

Ultimately, our shared humanity and the principles embedded within it hold the key to a future marked by unity, compassion, and prosperity. May this book serve as a guiding light on our journey toward a more enlightened and harmonious existence where the true spirit of humanity prevails.